Data Structures in Java

Top 100 Programming Questions and Solutions

Venkateswarlu Chennareddy

Feb 2024

To my family and friends

Contents

List of Figures

Listings

Preface

Welcome to an exploration of the fundamental building blocks of computer science and software development. Our journey begins with an introduction to **Data Structures**, the backbone of efficient programming. In this opening chapter, we embark on a quest to understand how data can be organized, managed, and stored in a way that enhances computational efficiency. Whether you're a beginner or looking to refresh your knowledge, this chapter sets the stage for the profound impact that well-chosen data structures have on the performance and scalability of software applications.

The second chapter delves into the world of **Arrays**, one of the simplest yet most powerful data structures available. Arrays provide a foundational understanding of how data can be sequentially organized and efficiently accessed. This chapter not only explores the basics of arrays but also introduces the reader to the complexities of array operations, laying the groundwork for more advanced data structures and algorithms that you will encounter later in the book.

Strings, often considered the first acquaintance programmers have with data structures, are the focus of our third chapter. Strings are pivotal in representing and manipulating text-based data. This chapter highlights the intricacies of string operations, from creation to manipulation, and the role strings play in communication within and between software systems. By demystifying strings, we offer readers a gateway to understanding more complex strings related techniques.

In Chapter Four, we unravel the complexities of **Hash Maps**, a data structure that champions speed and efficiency in data retrieval. By using the hashing techniques, this chapter illuminates the critical role hash maps play in modern software development, especially in applications requiring rapid access to large datasets, like databases and caching systems.

Recursion, a concept that often puzzles newcomers, is elegantly unfolded in our fifth chapter. **Recursion** is presented not just as a theoretical concept but as a practical programming tool, demonstrated through classic problems and algorithms. This chapter aims to transform recursion from a topic of apprehension to one of fascination, showcasing its power in simplifying complex problems by breaking them down into more manageable sub-problems.

The narrative then advances to **Linked Lists** in the sixth chapter, where we explore the dynamic nature of data structures. Unlike arrays, linked lists offer flexibility in data management, allowing for efficient insertions and deletions.

This chapter provides a comprehensive guide to understanding and implementing linked lists, highlighting their advantages and trade-offs compared to other data structures.

Our seventh chapter focuses on **Stacks and Queues**, data structures that are essential for managing data in specific order constraints. Through practical examples and real-world applications, this chapter elucidates the Last In, First Out (LIFO) principle of stacks and the First In, First Out (FIFO) principle of queues. Understanding these data structures is crucial for grasping concepts like task scheduling, parsing, and many more.

Finally, the book culminates with an exploration of **Binary Trees**, introducing readers to the hierarchical organization of data. This eighth chapter ventures into the realm of non-linear data structures, explaining how binary trees facilitate efficient traversal techniques. Through binary trees, readers will appreciate the depth and breadth of data structure applications, setting the stage for further exploration into more complex tree structures and graph-based algorithms.

Each chapter of this book has been carefully crafted to build upon the last, ensuring a cohesive and comprehensive understanding of data structures and algorithms. Through this journey, we aim to equip you with the knowledge and skills to tackle real-world problems with confidence and creativity. Welcome to the fascinating world of computer science, where every chapter unfolds new possibilities and insights.

Acknowledgements

Writing this book has been a journey that stretched beyond the confines of my personal capabilities and into the vast expanse of support and encouragement offered by those around me. It is with a heart full of gratitude that I take this moment to acknowledge the invaluable contributions of everyone who stood by me through this endeavor.

First and foremost, my deepest appreciation goes to my family. To my parents, whose belief in my abilities has been the cornerstone of my strength; to my wife, for her endless patience and understanding; and to my children, whose smiles light up my darkest days. You all are my inspiration and motivation.

A special note of thanks is reserved for my **Peer Reviewers** and **Editorial Reviewers**, whose keen insights and constructive criticism were instrumental in refining this book. Chun Yao, Narasimha Karumanchi, Kazuyuki Tanimura, Kousikan Veeramuthu, Ravi Dhanekula, Sateesh Naidu, Srinivas Pokuri, Rangarao Tumati, Sudheer Mupparaju, Radha Krishna Manam, Sujayendran S, Chandu Koppula, Praveen Kantipudi, Pavan Muppa, Manikantan M, Sravan Thokala, Anil Vemulapalli, Vamshi Krishna A, Manivannan D, and many others whose vigilant eyes missed nothing - your contributions have been invaluable.

I am also immensely grateful to **Shroff Publishers** and Distributors Pvt Ltd for bringing the Indian print version of this book to life. Your faith in this project and your commitment to excellence have been a source of constant encouragement.

Last but certainly not least, I wish to extend my heartfelt thanks to all my friends and well-wishers. Your support and guidance have been a ray of light, guiding me through the process of creating this book. It is difficult to put into words how much your encouragement has meant to me, but I hope this acknowledgment serves as a testament to my appreciation.

To everyone who has been a part of this journey, thank you from the bottom of my heart. Your support has not only helped bring this book into being but has also enriched my life in countless ways.

Chapter 1

Introduction

1.1 Data Structures

In computer science and programming, a data structure is a specialized format for organizing, processing, managing and storing the data efficiently.

There are several types of data structures. Different types of data structures are suited for different kinds of applications, and some are highly specialized to specific tasks. For example, arrays for storing and retrieving the data efficiently, Linked Lists for handling dynamic data sizes, Stacks for parsing and syntax checking of programming languages, Queues for handling tasks in a specific order, and Hash tables to look up the data.

1.2 Computational Complexity

In computer science, the computational complexity or simply complexity of an algorithm is the amount of resources required to run it. Particular focus is given to computation time and memory storage requirements. The study of the complexity of explicitly given algorithms is called analysis of algorithms, while the study of the complexity of problems is called computational complexity theory.

In general, there is always more than one way to solve a problem in computer science with different data structures and algorithms. so, it is required to use a method to compare the solutions in order to judge which one is more efficient. There are two such methods, time complexity and space complexity which we will discuss below:

1.2.1 Time Complexity

The time complexity is a type of computational complexity that describes the time required to execute an algorithm. The time complexity of an algorithm is the amount of time it takes for each statement to complete. As a result, it is highly dependent on the size of the processed data.

The time complexity is commonly expressed using big O notation, $O(n)$, $O(n \log n)$, $O(n^2)$, etc., where n is the size in units of bits needed to represent the input.

1.2.2 Space Complexity

The amount of memory required by the algorithm (or program) including the space of input values for execution to solve a given problem is called space complexity of the algorithm (or program).

Similar to time complexity, space complexity is often expressed asymptotically in big O notation, such as $O(n)$, $O(n \log n)$, $O(n^2)$, etc., where n is a characteristic of the input influencing space complexity.

1.3 Arrays

An array is a linear data structure that holds a fixed number of same data type and stores them in contiguous and adjacent memory locations. The length of an array is established when the array is created. After creation, its length is fixed. Arrays work on an index system starting from 0 to (n-1), where n is the size of the array.

Each item in an array is called an element, and each element is accessed by its numerical index. As shown in the Figure 1.1, numbering begins with 0. For example, the 9th element is accessed at index 8.

This a way to declare an array (named anArray) with the following line of code in Java:

```
//declares an array of integers
int[] anArray;
```

1.4 Strings

A string is a data type that is used to represent the text. A string is a collection of characters surrounded by double quotes. It can contain letters, numbers, symbols and even spaces.

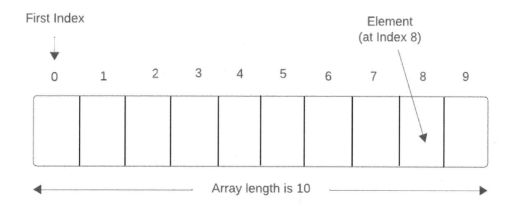

Figure 1.1: An array of 10 elements

The most direct way to create a string is to write:

```
String greeting = "Hello world!";
```

In this case, "Hello world!" is a string literal — a series of characters in your code that is enclosed in double quotes.

1.5   Recursion

Recursion is a method of solving a computational problem where the solution depends on solutions to smaller instances of the same problem. Some of the most common examples for recursion are computing Fibonacci sequence, computing factorials, merge sort and the Towers of Hanoi.

1.6   Hash Table

Hash Table is a data structure that provide fast retrieval of values based on keys. It stores the data in (Key, Value) pairs. Any non-null object can be used as a key or as a value. To successfully store and retrieve objects from a hash table, the objects used as keys must implement the hashCode method and the equals method.

Declaration of HashMap and HashTable in Java:

```
//Declare a Hashtable
Hashtable<String, Integer> hashtable = new Hashtable<>();
```

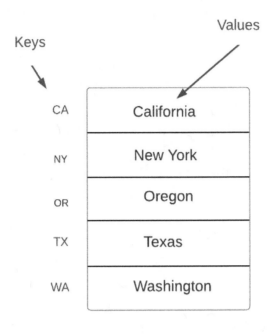

Figure 1.2: Hash Table or Hash Map

1.7 Hash Map

Hash Map, is similar to Hash Table, is a data structure that stores the data in (Key, Value) pairs but it is un-synchronized. It allows to store the null keys as well, but there should be only one null key object and there can be any number of null values.

```
// Declare a HashMap
HashMap<String, Integer> map = new HashMap<>();
```

Both Hash tables and Hash Maps use a hashing function to map keys to indexes in an array, allowing for constant-time access in the average case. Hash tables are commonly used in dictionaries, caches, and database indexing. However, hash collisions can occur, which can impact their performance. Techniques like separate chaining and open addressing are employed to handle collisions.

1.8 Linked Lists

A linked list is a linear collection of data elements of any type, called nodes, where each node has itself a value (element), and pointer (next) to the next node in the linked list. The main advantage of a linked list over an array is that values can always be efficiently inserted and removed without relocating the rest of the list. Certain other operations, such as random access to a certain element, are however slower on lists than on arrays.

This a way to declare a LinkedList with the following line of code in Java:

```
//declare a LinkedList
LinkedList list = new LinkedList();
```

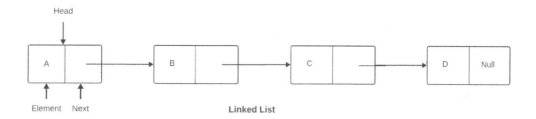

Figure 1.3: A Linked List of 4 nodes

1.9 Stacks

A Stack is a linear data structure that serves as a collection of elements with the following main operations:

- Push, adds an element to the collection

- Pop, removes the most recently added element

- Peek, return the value of the last element added without modifying the stack

The name stack is an analogy to a set of physical items stacked one atop another, such as a stack of plates.

The order in which an element added to or removed from a stack is described as **L**ast **I**n, **F**irst **O**ut, most frequently referred as **LIFO**.

1.10 Queues

A queue is a linear data structure where elements are stored in the First In First Out(FIFO) principle. The following are main operations in a Queue:

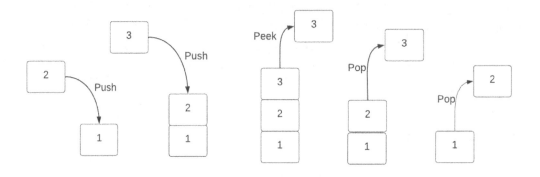

Figure 1.4: Stack Operations

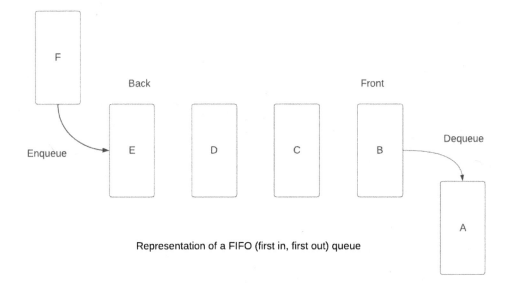

Representation of a FIFO (first in, first out) queue

Figure 1.5: Queue Operations

- enqueue, adds an element to the rear of the queue

- dequeue, deletes an element from the front

- Peek (or front operation), returns the value of the next element to be dequeued without dequeuing it

The first element added to the queue will be the first one to be removed. This is equivalent to the requirement that once a new element is added, all elements that were added before have to be removed before the new element can be removed.

The data is inserted into the queue through one end (rear) and deleted from it using the other end (front) where as in stack both operations at one end.

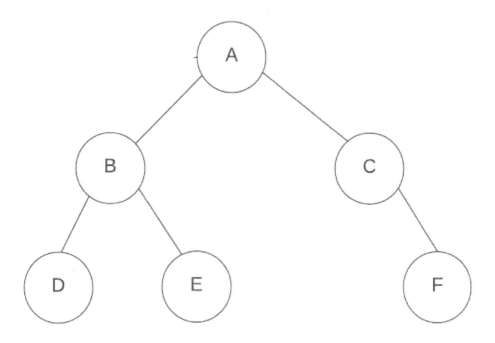

Figure 1.6: Binary Tree

1.11 Binary Trees

A tree is a nonlinear data structure, compared to arrays, linked lists, stacks and queues which are linear data structures. A tree can be empty with no nodes or a tree is a structure consisting of one node called the root and zero or one or more sub-trees.

A binary tree is the specialized version of a general tree. A binary tree is a tree with a maximum of two children for each parent node. Each node in a binary tree has a left and right reference along with the data element. The node at the top of the tree is called a root node. The nodes that hold other sub-nodes are the parent nodes. The nodes that have no children are called leaf nodes.

Chapter 2

Arrays

2.1 Introduction

Array is a data structure that is used to store the elements of the same data type in a sequential fashion. For example,

```
int[] a = {1, 2, 3, 4, 5};               // Array of numbers
String[] str1 = {"How", "are" "you"};    // Array of Strings
```

Listing 2.1: Arrays example

2.2 Majority Element

2.2.1 Problem

Write a program which takes an array and print a majority element if it exists. Otherwise, print None.

A majority element in an array A[] of size n is an element that appears more than n/2 times.

Example 1:
Input : {3, 3, 4, 2, 4, 4, 2, 4, 4}
Output : 4

Example 2:
Input : {3, 3, 4, 2, 4, 4, 2, 4}
Output : None

2.2.2 Algorithm

Step 1: Find a Candidate for Majority Element

1. Initialize two variables: count to 0 and major to store the index of a potential majority element.
2. Iterate through each element a[i] in the array a.

- If count is 0, set major to the current element a[i] and set count to 1.

- If the current element a[i] is equal to major, increment count.

- Otherwise, decrement count.

3. After completing the iteration, major will hold a candidate for the majority element. However, this step does not guarantee that the candidate is indeed a majority element, as count could represent a balance between different elements rather than a majority.

Step 2: Verify the Candidate is a Majority Element

1. Initialize a new count variable to 0 and obtain the size of the array size.
2. Iterate through each element a[i] in the array a.

- If the current element a[i] is equal to the candidate majNum, increment count.

3. After completing the iteration, check if count is greater than size/2.

- If count > size/2, then majNum is indeed a majority element, and the function returns true.

- Otherwise, it returns false, indicating that no majority element exists in the array.

2.2.3 Program

```java
public class MajorityElement {

    // Step 1 : Find majority element
    private int findMajority(int[] a) {
        int count = 0, major = 0;
        for (int i = 0; i < a.length; i++) {
            if (count == 0) {
                major = a[i];
                count = 1;
            } else if (a[i] == major) {
                count++;
```

```
13            } else {
14                count--;
15            }
16        }
17        return major;
18    }
19
20    /* Step 2: Verify that number returned in step 1 is a
       majority element */
21    private boolean isMajority(int[] a, int majNum) {
22        int count = 0, size = a.length;
23        for (int i = 0; i < size; i++) {
24            if (a[i] == majNum) {
25                count++;
26            }
27        }
28        return (count > size / 2) ? true : false;
29    }
30
31    // Print majority element if any. Otherwise, print None
32    private void printMajority(int[] a) {
33        int majorityNum = findMajority(a);
34        System.out.println(isMajority(a, majorityNum) ?
35                majorityNum : "None");
36    }
37
38    public static void main(String[] args) {
39        int[] a = {3, 3, 4, 2, 4, 4, 2, 4, 4};
40        MajorityElement m = new MajorityElement();
41        m.printMajority(a);
42    }
43 }
```

Listing 2.2: Majority Element

2.2.4 Analysis

This program efficiently finds a majority element in two passes over the array:

- The first pass selects a candidate using the Boyer-Moore voting algorithm principle, which relies on the count balance between the potential majority element and the rest of the array.

- The second pass verifies that the selected candidate is indeed a majority element by counting its occurrences in the array and comparing it to half the array's size.

This approach ensures a **time complexity** of O(n) and a **space complexity** of O(1), making it an efficient solution for finding the majority element in an array.

2.3 Binary Search

2.3.1 Problem

Write a program for a Binary Search.

Binary search is an efficient well-known algorithm for finding an item in a sorted list of items. It works by repeatedly dividing in half the portion of the list that could contain the item until we narrowed down to one item.

The time Complexity of Binary Search Algorithm is O(log n).

Example 1:
Input : a = { 1, 5, 9, 12}, k=5
Output : 1

Example 2:
Input : a = {1, 4, 7, 9, 10, 12, 18, 24, 28, 30}, k=30
Output : 9

2.3.2 Algorithm

Step 1: Initialize Variables

- Set `low` to 0 (the first index of the array).

- Set `high` to `a.length` - 1 (the last index of the array).

Step 2: Loop Until the Search Space is Valid

While `low` is less than or equal to `high`, do the following steps:

Step 3: Calculate the Midpoint

Calculate `mid` as `low + (high - low) / 2`. This prevents integer overflow that could occur from `(low + high) / 2`.

Step 4: Compare the Target Value with the Midpoint

- If the target value `k` is less than the value at `a[mid]`, narrow the search to the left half by setting `high` to `mid - 1`.

- If the target value `k` is greater than the value at `a[mid]`, narrow the search to the right half by setting `low` to `mid + 1`.

- If the target value k equals the value at a[mid], the target has been found. Return mid as the index where the target is located.

Step 5: Target Not Found

If the while loop exits without returning an index, this indicates that the target value k is not present in the array. Return -1 to indicate the absence of the target value.

2.3.3 Program

```
public int BinarySearch(int[] a, int k) {
    int low, mid, high;
    low=0; high=a.length;

    while (low <= high) {
        mid = low + (high-low)/2;
        if(k < a[mid]) {
            high = mid-1;
        }
        else if(k > a[mid]) {
            low = mid+1;
        }
        else {
            return mid;
        }
    }

    return -1;
}
```

Listing 2.3: Binary Search

2.3.4 Analysis

Time Complexity

- Best Case: O(1) - This occurs when the target value is at the midpoint of the entire array during the first comparison.

- Average and Worst Case: $O(\log_2 n)$ - Each step of the binary search algorithm divides the search space in half, leading to a logarithmic number of steps. Therefore, for an array of size n, the maximum number of steps required will be $O(\log_2 n)$.

Space Complexity

- $O(1)$ - Binary search is performed in place, and the space used by the algorithm is constant, regardless of the size of the input array. The only extra space used is for the few variables (low, high, mid, and k), which occupy a constant amount of space.

Advantages

- Highly efficient for searching in sorted arrays, significantly faster than linear search for large datasets.

Disadvantages

- The array must be sorted prior to performing a binary search, which could be costly if the array is not already sorted.

- Not suitable for searching in unsorted arrays or linked lists where elements are not sequentially accessible.

2.4 Balanced Parenthesis

2.4.1 Problem

Write a program to check if the given expression contains balanced parenthesis.

Example 1:
Input : a-((b+c)*d)+e
Output : true

Example 2:
Input : (a+b)*c)
Output : false

2.4.2 Algorithm

Step 1: Initialize the Counter

- Start by initializing a counter variable **count** to 0. This counter will keep track of the balance of parentheses.

Step 2: Iterate through the String

- Loop through each character of the string using a **for** loop. For each iteration, check the current character.

Step 3: Increment for Open Parenthesis

- If the current character is an open parenthesis ')(', increment the `count` by 1. This signifies that a new set of parentheses has been opened.

Step 4: Decrement for Close Parenthesis

- If the current character is a close parenthesis ')', decrement the `count` by 1. This signifies that a previously opened set of parentheses has been closed.

Step 5: Early Termination Check

- After each decrement, check if `count` becomes negative. If `count` is negative, it means a closing parenthesis has appeared without a corresponding opening parenthesis before it, making the parentheses imbalanced. Return `false` immediately.

Step 6: Final Check for Balance

- After the loop ends, check if `count` is equal to 0. If `count` is 0, it means every opening parenthesis has a corresponding closing parenthesis, and the parentheses are balanced. Return `true`.

Step 7: Unbalanced Parentheses

- If `count` is not 0, it means there are opening parentheses without corresponding closing ones, making the parentheses imbalanced. The function will return `false` as a result of the final check.

2.4.3 Program

```java
public boolean isBalanceParenthesis(String str){
    int count = 0;
    for(int i=0; i < str.length(); i++) {
      if(str.charAt(i) == '(') {
        count++;
      }
      else if(str.charAt(i) == ')') {
        count--;
      }
      if(count<0){
        return false;
      }
    }
    return count == 0;
  }
```

Listing 2.4: Balanced Parenthesis

2.4.4 Analysis

Time Complexity

- O(n): The time complexity of this algorithm is linear, where **n** is the length of the input string. This is because the algorithm iterates through each character of the string exactly once.

Space Complexity

- O(1): The space complexity is constant because the algorithm uses a fixed amount of space (the `count` variable) regardless of the input size.

2.4.5 Applications

- This simple algorithm is fundamental in compilers and text editors for validating the syntax of codes and documents that use parentheses for grouping.

- It can also be extended to check for balance and correct placement of various types of brackets and symbols in mathematical expressions and programming languages.

2.5 Check Rotation

2.5.1 Problem

Given two strings str1 and str2, write a program to check str2 is rotation of str1

Example 1:
Input : abcde cdeab
Output : true

Example 2:
Input : abcde cdeba
Output : false

2.5.2 Algorithm

1. Initialization: Start by taking two strings **str1** and **str2** as input. The goal is to check if **str2** is a rotation of **str1**.

2. Check for Substring (isSubstring method):

- For each possible start position in str1 (from 0 to m-n+1, where m is the length of str1 and n is the length of str2), do the following:

    - Compare each character of a substring of str1 starting from the current start position with the corresponding character in str2.

    - If any character does not match, break out of the inner loop and move to the next start position in str1.

    - If all characters match (i.e., reached the end of str2 without breaking), return true indicating str2 is a substring of str1.

- If no start position leads to a match, return false.

3. Check for Rotation (isRotation method):

- Concatenate str1 with itself and store it in a new string temp.

- Use the isSubstring method to check if str2 is a substring of temp.

- Return the result of the isSubstring method.

4. Execution:

- In the main method, create an instance of the CheckRotation class and use the isRotation method to check if str2 is a rotation of str1.

- Print the result.

2.5.3 Program

```
1  public class CheckRotation {
2
3    boolean isSubstring(String str1, String str2)
4    {
5      int m=str1.length(), n=str2.length();
6      for(int i=0; i<m-n+1; i++) {
7        for(int j=0; j<n; j++) {
8          if(str1.charAt(i+j)!=str2.charAt(j)) {
9            break;
10         }
11         else if(j==n-1) {
12           return true;
```

17

```
13            }
14          }
15        }
16      return false;
17    }
18
19    boolean isRotation(String str1, String str2)
20    {
21        // Concatenate str1+str1
22        String temp=str1+str1;
23
24        // Check str2 is a substring of temp
25        return isSubstring(temp, str2);
26
27    }
28
29    public static void main(String[] args) {
30        CheckRotation r = new CheckRotation();
31        String str1="abcde";
32        String str2="cdeab";
33        System.out.println(r.isRotation(str1, str2));
34    }
35 }
```

Listing 2.5: Check Rotation

2.5.4 Analysis

Time Complexity

- The isSubstring method has a nested loop structure where the outer loop runs for m-n+1 iterations (where m is the length of str1 and n is the length of str2), and the inner loop runs for up to n iterations in the worst case. Thus, the time complexity of isSubstring is $O((m-n+1)n)$, which simplifies to $O(mn)$ in the worst case.

- The isRotation method concatenates str1 with itself, which is an $O(m)$ operation, and then calls isSubstring on the concatenated string and str2. Since the length of the concatenated string is 2m, the call to isSubstring has a time complexity of $O(2mn)$, which simplifies to $O(mn)$.

- Therefore, the overall time complexity of the algorithm is $O(mn)$.

Space Complexity

- The space complexity is mainly determined by the temporary string `temp` used to store the concatenation of `str1` with itself, which takes $O(m)$ space, where `m` is the length of `str1`.

- The `isSubstring` method uses constant space for its indices and loop variables.

- Thus, the overall space complexity of the algorithm is $O(m)$.

2.6   Compact Spaces

2.6.1   Problem

Write a program to replace multiple spaces with a single space in a given string

```
Example 1:
 Input : Hello    how   are    you
 Output : Hello how are you

Example 2:
 Input : H      e   ll     o
 Output : H e l l o
```

2.6.2   Algorithm

1. Convert the Input String to Character Array

   - Convert the input string `str` into a character array `arr` to process each character individually.

2. Initialize Two Pointers

   - Initialize two pointers, `i` and `j`, both set to 0. Pointer `i` tracks the position to insert the next non-space character (or single space between words), and `j` is used to iterate through the array.

3. Iterate through the Character Array

Using a loop, iterate through the array with pointer j. For each character:

- Check if the current character `arr[j]` is not a space, or it is the last character in the array, or the next character `arr[j+1]` is not a space.

- If the condition is true, copy `arr[j]` to `arr[i]`, and increment i.

4. Create a New String

- After the loop completes, create a new string from the character array `arr` starting from index 0 up to index i (exclusive), effectively compressing consecutive spaces to a single space.

2.6.3 Program

```
String CompressSpaces(String str)
  {
    char[] arr = str.toCharArray();
    int i=0, j=0;
    for(; j<arr.length; j++) {
      if(arr[j] != ' ' || (j+1==arr.length) || arr[j+1] !=
      ' ') {
        arr[i++]=arr[j];
      }
    }
    return String.valueOf(arr, 0, i);
  }
```

Listing 2.6: Compact Spaces

2.6.4 Analysis

Time Complexity

- O(n): The algorithm iterates through each character of the input string exactly once, where **n** is the length of the input string. Therefore, the time complexity is linear, O(n).

Space Complexity

- O(n): The algorithm uses an additional character array `arr` of the same size as the input string to manipulate and eventually create the compressed string. Thus, the space complexity is linear, O(n), due to the extra storage required for the character array.

This program efficiently compresses consecutive spaces into a single space in a given string with optimal time and space complexity.

2.7   Intersection of two sorted arrays

2.7.1   Problem

Write a program to find intersection of two sorted arrays.

Example
Input :
a = {4, 4, 5, 5, 6, 8, 9}
b = {4, 5, 5, 6, 8, 9}
Output : 4, 5, 6, 8, 9

2.7.2   Algorithm

1. Initialize Pointers

- Start with two pointers, i and j, both set to 0. These pointers are used to iterate through the two sorted arrays a and b respectively.

2. Initialize a Variable for Last Match:

- Initialize a variable `lastMatch` to store the last matched element to avoid printing duplicates. Initially, it can be set to a value that is not possible to appear in the arrays (e.g., the smallest possible value).

3. Iterate through Both Arrays:

- Use a while loop to continue iteration as long as both pointers i and j are within the bounds of their respective arrays.

4. Check for Matching Elements

- Inside the loop, check if the current elements pointed by i and j are equal and also ensure that this element is not the same as lastMatch to avoid printing duplicate elements. If a match is found, update lastMatch with this value, print the matched element, and increment both i and j.

5. Advance Pointers

- If the current element in array a is less than the current element in array b, increment i to move to the next element in a.

- Conversely, if the current element in a is greater, increment j to move to the next element in b.

- This step ensures that the algorithm efficiently finds matches by exploiting the sorted nature of the arrays.

6. Terminate Upon Completion

- The loop terminates when either array has been completely traversed, ensuring all possible matches have been found and printed.

2.7.3 Program

```java
void IntersectionOfTwoSortedArrays(int[] a, int[] b) {
    int i=0, j=0;
    int lastMatch = 0;
    // Iterate through the arrays and print common elements
    while(i<a.length && j<b.length){
        if(a[i]==b[j] && a[i]!=lastMatch){
            lastMatch = a[i];
            System.out.print(a[i]+" ");
            i++;
            j++;
        }
        else if(a[i]<b[j]){
            i++;
        }
        else{
            j++;
        }
    }
}
```

Listing 2.7: Intersection of two sorted arrays

2.7.4 Analysis

Time Complexity

O(n+m): The algorithm iterates through each array at most once, where n and m are the lengths of arrays a and b respectively. The while loop runs until the end of one of the arrays is reached, making the time complexity linear in the size of the input arrays.

Space Complexity

O(1): No extra space is used besides a few variables for iteration control and storing the last matched element, making the space complexity constant, O(1). This algorithm efficiently finds and prints the intersection of two sorted arrays without duplicates, leveraging the sorted order to minimize the number of comparisons and ensuring optimal time and space complexity.

2.8 Decimal to Roman

2.8.1 Problem

Write a program to convert a decimal to roman number

Example 1:
Input : 4919
Output : MMMMCMXIX

Example 2:
Input : 4
Output : IV

2.8.2 Algorithm

1. Define Roman Numerals and Their Values

   - Create two arrays: `RomanCode` holds the Roman numeral symbols in descending order of value, and `DecimalVal` holds the corresponding decimal values.

2. Initialize an Empty StringBuilder

- Use a `StringBuilder` named `roman` to accumulate the resulting Roman numeral string.

3. Convert Decimal to Roman

- Iterate through the `DecimalVal` array using an index i. For each value, check if the input decimal number is greater than or equal to `DecimalVal[i]`.

    - While this condition is true, subtract `DecimalVal[i]` from the decimal number and append the corresponding `RomanCode[i]` to the `StringBuilder`.

    - This process is repeated until the decimal number is reduced to 0.

4. Return the Roman Numeral String

- Convert the `StringBuilder` to a `String` and return it as the final Roman numeral representation.

2.8.3   Program

```
public String decimalToRoman(int decimal) {
  String[] RomanCode = {"M", "CM", "D", "CD", "C", "XC", "
    L", "XL", "X", "IX", "V", "IV", "I"};
  int[] DecimalVal = {1000, 900, 500, 400, 100, 90, 50,
    40, 10, 9, 5, 4, 1};

  // Roman notation will be accumulated here.
  StringBuilder roman = new StringBuilder();
  /* Loop from biggest value to smallest, successively
    subtracting, from the binary value while adding to the
    roman representation. */
  for (int i = 0; i < RomanCode.length; i++) {
    while (decimal >= DecimalVal[i]) {
      decimal -= DecimalVal[i];
      roman.append(RomanCode[i]);
    }
  }
  return roman.toString();
}
```

Listing 2.8: Decimal to Roman

2.8.4 Analysis

Time Complexity

$O(1)$: Although the algorithm involves a loop, the number of iterations is capped by the size of the `RomanCode` and `DecimalVal` arrays, which are fixed and independent of the input size. Thus, the time complexity is considered constant. Note that the number of iterations for subtracting and appending in the worst case is proportional to the input value, but since Roman numerals have a maximum defined by the largest symbol ($M = 1000$), this does not significantly affect the overall time complexity for inputs within the range of representable values.

Space Complexity

$O(1)$: The additional space used by the algorithm is limited to the `StringBuilder` and a few variables for iteration, which do not grow with the size of the input number. The arrays `RomanCode` and `DecimalVal` are fixed in size. Thus, the space complexity is also considered constant.

Summary

This algorithm efficiently converts a decimal number to its Roman numeral representation using a systematic approach that matches decimal values to their closest Roman numeral counterparts and builds the numeral string progressively.

2.9 Find Leaders

2.9.1 Problem

Write a program find all the leaders in an array. An element a[i] is a leader if all the elements right side of this is smaller than a[i] value.

Example 1:
Input : 7, 2, 3, 5, 2, 3, 1
Output : 1 3 5 7

Example 2:
Input : 1, 1, 9, 4, 6, 2, 5
Output : 5 6 9

2.9.2 Algorithm

(a) Initialize Variables:

- Determine the array length **n**.
- Set **max** to the last element of the array (**a[n-1]**) since the last element is always a leader.

(b) Print the Last Element: Print the last element of the array as it is considered a leader.

(c) Iterate Backwards through the Array:

- Start from the second last element (index **n-2**) and iterate back to the first element (index 0).
- For each element, compare it with **max**. If the current element **a[i]** is greater than **max**, it is a leader.

(d) Update and Print Leaders: Upon finding a leader, print its value and update **max** to this new leader's value.

(e) End of Algorithm: The process continues until all elements have been compared, identifying all leaders in the array.

2.9.3 Program

```java
public void findLeaders(int[] a)
{
    int n=a.length;
    int max=a[n-1];
    // last value (right most) is always leader as there are no more values after that on right side
    System.out.print(max + " ");
    // Go from right to left and print all the maximum values (leaders)
    for(int i=n-2; i>=0; i--) {
        if(a[i]>max){
            System.out.print(a[i] + " ");
            max=a[i];
        }
    }
}
```

Listing 2.9: Find Leaders

2.9.4 Analysis

Time Complexity

O(n): The algorithm iterates through the array once, from the end to the beginning. The number of operations is proportional to the length of the array n, making the time complexity linear.

Space Complexity

O(1): The space used by the algorithm is constant. It only requires a fixed amount of extra space for variables n, max, and the loop index i, regardless of the input size.

This program efficiently identifies leaders in an array by checking from right to left, ensuring that each element is greater than all the elements to its right, and utilizes constant extra space for its operations.

2.10 Maximum Loss

2.10.1 Problem

Given an array of stock prices from day 0 to N-1 of a company X, find out the max loss that is possible. Loss occurs if stock is bought at higher price and sold at lower price.

Example 1:
Input : 1 2 3 7 5 8 9 4 6 10 12
Output : 5
Max Loss is 9-4=5 (Possible losses are 8-4=4, 7-5=2 etc)
Max difference between stock price is 12-1=11 but max loss is 9-4=5

Example 2:
Input : 10, 2, 3, 13, 5, 8
Output : 8

2.10.2 Algorithm

1. Initialize Variables

- Initialize `max` to the first element of the array (`a[0]`) to keep track of the maximum stock price seen so far.

- Initialize `maxLoss` to 0 to track the maximum loss.

2. Iterate through the Array

- Start iterating from the second element (index 1) to the end of the array.

3. Calculate Loss

- For each element `a[i]`, calculate the difference between `max` and `a[i]` to find the current loss.

4. Update Maximum Loss

- If the current loss (`max - a[i]`) is greater than `maxLoss`, update `maxLoss` with the current loss.

5. Update Maximum Stock Price

- If the current element `a[i]` is greater than `max`, update `max` with `a[i]` to track the new maximum stock price seen so far.

6. Return Maximum Loss

- After iterating through the entire array, return `maxLoss` as the maximum stock loss encountered.

2.10.3 Program

```java
int maxStockLoss(int[] a)
{
    int max=a[0], maxLoss=0;
    for(int i=1; i<a.length; i++) {
        if(maxLoss < (max-a[i]) ){
            maxLoss = max-a[i];
        }
        if(max<a[i]){
            max=a[i];
        }
    }
    return maxLoss;
}
```

Listing 2.10: Maximum Loss

2.10.4 Analysis

Time Complexity

O(n): The algorithm iterates through the array once, where n is the number of elements in the array. The time complexity is linear, as the operations within the loop are constant time operations.

Space Complexity

O(1): The space used by the algorithm is constant. It only requires a fixed amount of extra space for variables `max`, `maxLoss`, and the loop index `i`, regardless of the input size.

Summary

This program efficiently calculates the maximum stock loss by keeping track of the maximum stock price seen so far and updating the maximum loss whenever a new loss exceeds the previous maximum loss, using only a single pass through the array and constant extra space.

2.11 Maximum Sub-sequence Sum

2.11.1 Problem

Find maximum sub-sequence sum from a given array of +ve and -ve numbers

Example 1:
Input : 10, -12, 10, -5, 15;
Output : 20

Example 2:
Input : 10, -12, 20, 5, -15, -10, 4, 7, 0, -11, 15
Output : 25

2.11.2 Algorithm

1. Initialize Variables

- Initialize two variables, tempSum and maxSum, to 0. tempSum is used to track the sum of the current subsequence, and maxSum is used to keep track of the maximum sum encountered so far.

2. Iterate through the Array

- Iterate through each element of the array a using a loop.

3. Update tempSum

- For each element a[i], update tempSum by adding the current element to the maximum of 0 and tempSum. This effectively resets tempSum to a[i] if tempSum becomes negative (ensuring only subsequences with a positive sum are considered).

4. Update maxSum

- If tempSum is greater than maxSum after the update, assign the value of tempSum to maxSum. This step ensures that the maximum sum of any subsequence is captured.

5. Return Maximum Sum

- After iterating through the entire array, return maxSum as the maximum sum of any subsequence.

2.11.3 Program

```
1
2    /* Find maximum subsequence sum from given array of +
     ve and -ve numbers */
3    int maxSubsequenceSum(int[] a) {
4      int tempSum, maxSum;
5      tempSum = maxSum = 0;
6      for(int i=0; i<a.length; i++) {
7            // reset value of tempSum with a[i] whenever
         it is -ve
8        tempSum = a[i] + max(0, tempSum);
9        if(tempSum > maxSum) {
10         maxSum = tempSum;
11       }
12     }
13     return maxSum;
14   }
15
16   //Find maximum of given two numbers
```

```
17    int max(int a, int b)
18    {
19      return a>b?a:b;
20    }
```

Listing 2.11: Maximum Sub-sequence Sum

2.11.4 Analysis

Time Complexity

$O(n)$: The program iterates through the array exactly once, where n is the number of elements in the array. Since all operations within the loop (including the call to max) are constant time, the overall time complexity is linear.

Space Complexity

$O(1)$: The space used by the program is constant, as it only requires a fixed amount of extra space for the variables tempSum, maxSum, and the loop index i, regardless of the input size.

This program efficiently finds the maximum sum of any subsequence in the given array by using a single pass through the array and maintaining a running sum that resets whenever it becomes negative, ensuring that only positive contributions to the sum are considered.

2.12 Palindrome Number

2.12.1 Problem

Write a program to check the given positive integer number is a palindrome or not.

A palindromic number is a number that remains the same when its reads from left to right or right to left. For example, 121

Example 1:
Input : 1221
Output : true

Example 2:
Input : 120012
Output : false

2.12.2 Algorithm

1. Handle Negative Numbers

   - Check if the input number n is negative. Since negative numbers cannot be palindromes due to the "-" sign, return false immediately for any negative input.

2. Initialize Divider

   - Initialize a divider div to 1. This divider is used to extract the leftmost digit of the number.

3. Calculate the Initial Divider

   - Use a loop to increase the value of div by a factor of 10 until n/div is less than 10. This ensures that div corresponds to the highest power of 10 less than or equal to n, effectively making div equal to the place value of the leftmost digit of n.

4. Check Palindrome

   - Use a while loop to check if the number n is a palindrome by comparing digits from the left and right ends moving towards the center. Continue the loop until n becomes 0. Extract the leftmost digit by dividing n by div.

     – Extract the rightmost digit by taking n
     – If the leftmost and rightmost digits are not the same, return false.
     – Remove the checked digits from n by updating n to (n%div)/10. This removes the leftmost digit by taking n%div and the rightmost digit by further dividing by 10.
     – Update div by dividing it by 100 to adjust for the removal of two digits from n.

5. Return Result

   - If the loop completes without finding mismatched digits, return true, indicating that n is a palindrome.

2.12.3 Program

```
boolean isPalindromeNumber(int n){
  if(n < 0) {
    return false;
  }
  else {
    int div=1;
    while(n/div >=10) {
      div *= 10;
    }

    while(n>0){
      int left = n/div;
      int right = n%10;
      if(left != right) {
        return false;
      }
      n = (n%div)/10;
      div /= 100;
    }
  }
  return true;
}
```

Listing 2.12: Palindrome Number

2.12.4 Analysis

Time Complexity

Finding the Divider: The loop to calculate div runs in O(log10(n)) time since div is multiplied by 10 until it is just smaller than n.

Palindrome Check: The while loop for checking if n is a palindrome also runs in $O(\log_{10} n)$ time since it effectively halves the number of digits in n at each step (by removing two digits at a time).

Overall, the time complexity of the program is $O(\log_{10} n)$,where n is the value of the input number.

Space Complexity

O(1): The program uses a fixed amount of extra space (a few integer variables: div, left, right, and the input n itself), independent of the input size. Therefore, the space complexity is constant.

2.13 Run Length

2.13.1 Problem

Find a run length of a given string. For example, run length for a string aaabcc is a3b1c2

Example 1:
Input : abcbbd
Output : a1b1c1b2d1

Example 2:
Input : aaabbdhhaac
Output : a3b2d1h2a2c1

2.13.2 Algorithm

1. Initialize a StringBuilder

   - Create a StringBuilder object sb to efficiently build the run-length encoded string.

2. Iterate Through the Input String:

   - Use a for loop to iterate through each character of the input string str.

3. Count Consecutive Characters:

   - Initialize runLength to 1 for the current character.

   - Use a while loop to check if the current character (str.charAt(i)) is the same as the next character (str.charAt(i+1)).

     - If they are the same, increment runLength and i to continue counting consecutive identical characters.

     - The loop continues until a different character is encountered or the end of the string is reached.

4. Append Character and Its Count to StringBuilder

   - After exiting the while loop, append the current character (str.charAt(i)) and its count (runLength) to the StringBuilder object sb.

5. Return the Encoded String:

- After the for loop completes, convert the StringBuilder object sb to a string and return it.

2.13.3 Program

```
public String runLengthAlgo(String str) {
StringBuilder sb = new StringBuilder();
for(int i=0; i<str.length(); i++) {
  int runLength=1;
  while(i+1<str.length() && str.charAt(i)==str.charAt(
i+1)){
    runLength++;
    i++;
  }
  sb.append(str.charAt(i)).append(runLength);
}
return sb.toString();
}
```

Listing 2.13: Run Length

2.13.4 Analysis

Time Complexity

O(n): The program iterates through each character of the input string exactly once. While there is a nested while loop, it does not result in more than a single pass through the string because the outer loop's index i is incremented inside the while loop for consecutive characters. Thus, each character is processed only once, leading to a linear time complexity.

Space Complexity

O(n): The space complexity is linear with respect to the input string's length. This is because the StringBuilder object sb may, in the worst case, grow to a size that is twice the length of the input string (for strings where no character repeats, resulting in each character being followed by the number '1'). However, in practical scenarios, especially for strings with many repeating characters, the size of the encoded string (sb) will be significantly less than twice the size of the input string.

2.14 Two Numbers Sum K

2.14.1 Problem

Write a program find any two numbers sum is equal to given number k in the array.

Example 1:
Input : a=1, 2, 3, 4 k=6
Output : 2 4

Example 2:
Input : a=18, 3, 21, 8, 10, 12, 67, 19, 20, 5, 35, 1 k=6
Output : 1 5

2.14.2 Algorithm

1. Sort the input array

   - Use Arrays.sort(a) to sort the input array a. This is necessary to apply the two-pointer technique effectively.

2. Initialize two pointers:

   - Initialize two pointers, i at the start of the array (0) and j at the end of the array (a.length-1).

3. Iterate and find the sum:

   - Use a for loop or while loop (with condition i < j) to iterate through the array with the two pointers.

   - Calculate the sum of the elements at the two pointers (int sum = a[i] + a[j]).

4. Check for the target sum (k)

   - If sum equals k, return true indicating that two numbers adding up to k have been found.

   - If sum is greater than k, decrement j to reduce the sum.

   - If sum is less than k, increment i to increase the sum.

5. Continue until the pointers meet

   - The loop continues until i is no longer less than j.

6. Return false if mo pair found

   - If the loop completes without returning true, return false indicating that no such pair was found.

2.14.3 Program

```
Boolean isTwoNumsSum(int[] a, int k) {
  // Sort the array using any O(nlogn) sorting technique
  Arrays.sort(a);
  int i,j;
  for(i=0,j=a.length-1; i<j; ){
    int sum = a[i]+a[j];
    if(sum == k) {
      //System.out.println(a[i] + " " + a[j]);
      return true;
    }
    else if(sum > k) {
      j--;
    }
    else {
      i++;
    }
  }
  //System.out.println("There are no two numbers sum
  will be " + k);
  return false;
}
```

Listing 2.14: Two Numbers Sum K

2.14.4 Analysis

Time Complexity

Sorting the Array: The Arrays.sort(a) method typically has a time complexity of O(n log n) for an array of length n.

Two-Pointer Technique: The subsequent for loop (or while loop) that scans the array from both ends towards the center has a linear time complexity, O(n), because each element is considered at most once.

Overall Time Complexity: The dominating factor here is the sorting step, so the overall time complexity is O(n log n).

Space Complexity

O(1): The program operates in-place with a constant amount of extra space. The space used by the sorting algorithm is not considered here as it depends on the implementation of Arrays.sort(). For the purpose of this analysis, aside from the input array itself, only a constant amount of additional space is used for the pointers and temporary variables, resulting in an overall space complexity of O(1).

2.15 Maximum Index Difference

2.15.1 Problem

Given an array arr[], find the maximum j–i such that arr[j] > arr[i]. For example,
arr = {1, 2, 3, 4, 5, 6}
output : 5 (j = 5, i = 0)
Example 1:
Input : {9, 2, 3, 4, 5, 6, 7, 8, 18, 0}
Output : 8

Example 2:
Input : {34, 8, 10, 3, 2, 80, 30, 33, 1}
Output : 6

2.15.2 Algorithm

1. Initialize Variables

   - maxDiff is initialized to track the maximum difference, i and j are used as indexes for iteration, and n stores the length of the array.

2. Create and Populate LMin and RMax Arrays

   - LMin Array: Starting from the left of the given array, fill LMin[] such that LMin[i] contains the minimum value from the start of the array up to i.

- RMax Array: Starting from the right of the given array, fill RMax[]
  such that RMax[j] contains the maximum value from j to the end
  of the array.

3. Traverse LMin and RMax Arrays

- Set i = 0 and j = 0, and start traversing both the LMin and RMax
  arrays simultaneously.

4. Find Maximum Index Difference

- While i < n and j < n, compare elements at LMin[i] and RMax[j].

  - If LMin[i] is less than RMax[j], calculate the difference (j-i),
    update maxDiff if this difference is greater than the current
    maxDiff, and then move j forward (j = j + 1) to check for a
    potentially greater difference.
  - If LMin[i] is not less than RMax[j], move i forward (i = i + 1)
    to find a smaller element that might allow a greater difference.

5. Continue Until End of Arrays

- The loop continues until either i or j reaches the end of their respective arrays.

6. Return maxDiff

- After completing the traversal, return the value of maxDiff as the
  maximum index difference.

2.15.3   Program

```
int maxIndexDiff(int arr[]) {
    int maxDiff, i ,j;
    int n = arr.length;

    int[] LMin = new int[n];
    int[] RMax = new int[n];

    // Construct LMin[] such that LMin[i] stores the min
    value from (arr[0] ..  arr[i])
    LMin[0] = arr[0];
    for (i = 1; i < n; ++i)
        LMin[i] = Math.min(arr[i], LMin[i-1]);
```

```
13
14      // Construct RMax[] such that RMax[j] stores the max
        value from (arr[j]..arr[n-1])
15      RMax[n-1] = arr[n-1];
16      for (j = n-2; j >= 0; --j)
17          RMax[j] = Math.max(arr[j], RMax[j+1]);
18
19      // Traverse both arrays from left to right to find
        optimum j - i
20      // This process is similar to merge() of MergeSort
21      i=0; j=0; maxDiff=-1;
22      while (j < n && i < n) {
23          if (LMin[i] < RMax[j]) {
24              maxDiff = Math.max(maxDiff, j-i);
25              j = j + 1;
26          }
27          else {
28              i = i+1;
29          }
30      }
31
32      return maxDiff;
33 }
```

Listing 2.15: Maximum Index Difference

2.15.4 Analysis

Time Complexity

$O(n)$: Constructing the LMin and RMax arrays each takes $O(n)$ time as each involves a single pass through the array of length n.
$O(n)$: The while loop that traverses the LMin and RMax arrays also takes at most $O(n)$ time since each of i and j can increment at most n times across both arrays.

Overall Time Complexity: The overall time complexity is $O(n) + O(n) + O(n) = O(n)$, considering the operations are sequential.

Space Complexity

$O(n)$: Additional space is required for the LMin and RMax arrays, each of size n.

Overall Space Complexity: The overall space complexity is $O(n)$ due to the storage requirements of the LMin and RMax arrays.

2.16   Trapping Rain Water

2.16.1   Problem

Given n non-negative integers representing an elevation map where the width of each bar is 1, write a program to compute how much water it is able to trap after raining.

Example 1:
Input : a = 0,1,0,2,1,0,1,3,2,1,2,1
Output : 6

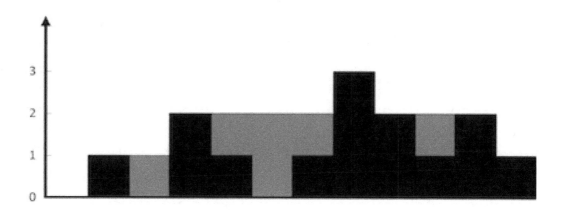

Figure 2.1: Trapping Rain Water

2.16.2   Algorithm

1. Initialization

   - Declare two arrays, left and right, of the same length as the input array A to store the maximum height of the wall to the left and right of each element, respectively.

   - Initialize a variable max to 0 for tracking the maximum height seen so far during iterations.

   - Check if the input array A is empty. If yes, return 0 as no water can be trapped.

2. Fill Left Max Array

- Iterate through the array A from left to right.

- Update max to be the maximum of max and the current element A[i].

- Assign max to left[i] to indicate the highest wall to the left of i.

3. Fill Right Max Array

- Reset max to 0 for the right pass.

- Iterate through the array A from right to left.

- Update max to be the maximum of max and the current element A[i].

- Assign max to right[i] to indicate the highest wall to the right of i.

4. Calculate Trapped Water

- Reset max to 0 to reuse it for calculating the total trapped water.

- Iterate through the array A from left to right.

- For each element i, calculate the trapped water above i by finding the minimum of left[i] and right[i] (which gives the effective boundary height) and subtracting the height of A[i] from it.

- Add the result to max, which now accumulates the total trapped water.

5. Return Total Trapped Water

- Return the accumulated total trapped water stored in max.

2.16.3 Program

```
int trap(int[] A) {
    int[] left=new int[A.length];
    int[] right=new int[A.length];
    if(A.length==0) return 0;
    int max=0;
    for(int i =0;i<A.length;i++){
        max=Math.max(max,A[i]);
        left[i]=max;
    }
    max=0;
```

```
11    for(int i =A.length-1;i>=0;i--){
12        max=Math.max(max,A[i]);
13        right[i]=max;
14    }
15    max=0;
16    for(int i =0;i<A.length;i++)
17        max+=Math.min(left[i],right[i])-A[i];
18    return max;
19    }
```

Listing 2.16: Trapping Rain Water

2.16.4   Analysis

Time Complexity

Filling the Left Max Array: O(n), where n is the length of the input array A. Each element is visited once.

Filling the Right Max Array: O(n), as it also involves a single pass through the array.

Calculating Trapped Water: O(n), since it requires iterating through the array once more.

Overall Time Complexity: O(n) + O(n) + O(n) = O(3n), which simplifies to O(n).

Space Complexity

Auxiliary Space: O(n) + O(n) for the left and right arrays, respectively.

Overall Space Complexity: O(2n), which simplifies to O(n).

Summary

This program efficiently calculates the total amount of water that can be trapped between the walls represented by the array A, utilizing dynamic programming concepts to precompute left and right boundaries for each element.

2.17 Next Greatest Number

2.17.1 Problem

Given an array of integers, replace every element with the next greatest element (greatest element on the right side) in the array. Since there is no element next to the last element, replace it with -1.

Example 1:
Input : 16, 17, 4, 3, 5, 2
Output : 17, 5, 5, 5, 2, -1

2.17.2 Algorithm

1. Initialization

   - Determine the length of the input array a and store it in n.

   - Initialize max with the value of the last element in the array a[n-1]. This is the greatest element to the right of the last element.

   - Replace the last element of the array a[n-1] with -1 as per the problem statement (since there is no element to the right of the last element).

2. Iterate Backwards through the Array

   - Starting from the second last element (index n-2), iterate backwards through the array towards the first element (index 0).

   - For each element i, store the current element a[i] in a temporary variable temp before modifying it.

   - Update a[i] to max. This operation replaces the current element with the greatest number found to its right so far.

   - Compare temp with max. If temp is greater than max, update max with temp. This step ensures max always contains the greatest element seen so far as we move leftward through the array.

3. Return the Modified Array

   - After completing the backward iteration, return the modified array a which now contains the greatest element to the right of each element.

2.17.3 Program

```
int[] replaceGreatestNumber(int[] a) {
    int n = a.length;
    int max = a[n-1];
    a[n-1] = -1;

    for(int i=n-2; i>=0; i--) {
        int temp = a[i];
        a[i] = max;
        if(temp > max) {
            max = temp;
        }
    }
    return a;
}
```

Listing 2.17: Next Greatest Number

2.17.4 Analysis

Time Complexity

The program makes a single pass through the array from right to left, performing constant-time operations for each element (comparisons, assignments).

Thus, the overall time complexity is O(n), where n is the number of elements in the input array.

Space Complexity

The modifications are done in-place, and no additional data structures of size proportional to the input array's size are used.
The space complexity is O(1), excluding the input array's space, as the algorithm only uses a fixed amount of additional space (max, temp, and loop indices).

Summary

This program efficiently replaces each element in the input array with the greatest element to its right using a single backward pass through the array, ensuring optimal time and space complexity.

Chapter 3

Strings

3.1 Introduction

A string is a data type that is used to represent the text. A string is a collection of characters surrounded by double quotes. It can contain letters, numbers, symbols and even spaces.

The most direct way to create a string is to write:

```
String greeting = "Hello world!";
```

In this case, "Hello world!" is a string literal — a series of characters in your code that is enclosed in double quotes.

3.2 Remove Duplicate Characters

3.2.1 Problem

Write a program to remove duplicate characters from a given string.

Example 1:
Input : ababac
Output : abc

Example 2:
Input : aabcbcdefdafg
Output : abcdefg

3.2.2 Algorithm

1. Convert String to Character Array

   - Convert the input string str into a character array arr to facilitate manipulation of individual characters.

2. Create a Hash table

   - Initialize a Hashtable named ht to track characters that have already been encountered. The key is of type Character, and the value is of type Boolean. Here, true indicates that the character has been encountered.

3. Iterate and Filter Duplicates

   - Use two pointers, i and j, where i tracks the position to insert a non-duplicate character, and j iterates through each character in arr.

   - For each character at position j, check if it is already present in ht. If it is not, it means the character is not a duplicate and can be added to the array at the position marked by i. Increment i to prepare for the next unique character.

   - Add each non-duplicate character encountered to ht with a value of true to mark its presence.

4. Convert Character Array Back to String

   - Convert the portion of the array from index 0 to i-1 (inclusive) back into a string. This portion of the array now contains only unique characters, with duplicates removed.

5. Return the Resulting String

   - Return the newly formed string with duplicates removed.

3.2.3 Program

```
String removeDuplcates(String str) {
    char[] arr = str.toCharArray();
    Hashtable<Character, Boolean> ht = new Hashtable<
    Character, Boolean>();
    int i, j;
    for( i=0, j=0; j<arr.length; j++) {
        if(ht.get(arr[j]) == null) {
            arr[i++]=arr[j];
            ht.put(arr[j], true);
        }
    }
    return String.valueOf(arr, 0, i);
}
```

Listing 3.1: Remove Duplicate Characters

3.2.4 Analysis

Time Complexity

O(n): The algorithm iterates through each character of the input string exactly once, where n is the length of the string. The operations within the loop (checking and inserting into a hashtable) are assumed to have average-case constant time complexity, O(1).

Therefore, the overall time complexity is linear with respect to the length of the input string.

Space Complexity

O(n): In the worst case, if all characters are unique, the hashtable ht will store an entry for each character. Additionally, the character array arr is a conversion of the input string and thus has a space complexity of O(n). However, since the question pertains to the extra space used by the algorithm beyond the input and output, the primary consideration is the space used by the hashtable.

The space complexity of the hashtable depends on the number of unique characters in the string. In the worst case (all characters are unique), this could be up to n, leading to a space complexity of O(n) for the hashtable.

Summary

This program efficiently removes duplicates from a string by utilizing a hashtable to track unique characters, ensuring both linear time and space complexity relative to the input size.

3.3 Rotate String

3.3.1 Problem

Write a program to rotate a given string right by k characters (k < size of given string)

Example 1:
Input : Hello, 2
Output : loHel

Example 2:
Input : Hello, 4
Output : elloH

3.3.2 Algorithm

1. Determine String Length:

   - Obtain the length n of the input string str.

2. Reverse Entire String

   - Call the reverse method on the entire string, which reverses the string from index 0 to n-1.

3. Reverse First k Characters

   - Call the reverse method on the first k characters of the reversed string, i.e., from index 0 to k-1. This step targets the last k characters of the original string due to the initial complete reversal.

4. Reverse the Rest of the String

   - Finally, reverse the portion of the string from index k to n-1. This action adjusts the positioning of the characters to achieve the desired right rotation.

3.3.3 Program

```
1    /**
2     * Reverse a string between i and j indexes
3     *
4     * @param str
5     * @param i
6     * @param j
7     * @return
8     */
9    String reverse(String str, int i, int j)
10   {
11      char[] arr = str.toCharArray();
12      for(;i<j; i++, j--) {
13         char temp = arr[i];
14         arr[i]=arr[j];
15         arr[j]=temp;
16      }
17      return String.valueOf(arr);
18   }
19
20   /**
21    * Rotate a string to right by k chars
22    *
23    * @param str
24    * @param k
25    */
26   String rotate(String str, int k)
27   {
28      int n = str.length();
29      //Reverse entire string
30      str = reverse(str, 0, n-1);
31      // Reverse first k characters in a string
32      str = reverse(str, 0, k-1);
33      // Reverse rest of the string
34      str = reverse(str, k, n-1);
35      return str;
36   }
```

Listing 3.2: Rotate String

3.3.4 Analysis

Time Complexity

$O(n)$: Each call to the reverse function iterates over a portion of the array, with a total of three calls. Despite these calls, each element is accessed a constant number of times, leading to an overall linear time complexity relative to the length of the input string.

Space Complexity

O(n): The space complexity is linear due to the conversion of the string to a character array (done inside the reverse method). This array is used to perform in-place character swaps. The space taken by this array is proportional to the length of the input string.

Summary

The method cleverly uses the principle that two reversals restore the original order of a subset of elements. By reversing the entire string, the method initially places the characters that are to be rotated to the front. Subsequent reversals of specific segments then correctly reposition these characters to simulate a rightward rotation by k characters.

3.4 Sub String

3.4.1 Problem

Write a program to check second string is a substring of first string

Example 1:
Input : str1="This is for testing" str2="testing";
Output : true

Example 2:
Input : str1="This is for testing" str2=" isor";
Output : false

3.4.2 Algorithm

1. Initialize lengths

   - Determine the lengths of strings a (assigned to m) and b (assigned to n).

2. Iterate through array

- Use a loop to iterate through string a with an index i, starting from 0 to m - n + 1. This ensures that the search only goes up to the point where the remaining characters in a are fewer than the length of b, preventing unnecessary comparisons.

3. Check for Substring

- For each position i in a, iterate through string b with an index j. Compare each character of b with the corresponding character in a starting from i.

  - If a character does not match, break the inner loop and move to the next position in a.
  - If all characters match (j reaches n-1), return true indicating b is a substring of a.

4. Return False

- If the end of a is reached without finding b as a substring, return false.

3.4.3 Program

```
Boolean isSubString(String a, String b) {
int m=a.length(), n=b.length();
for(int i=0; i<m-n+1; i++) {
  for(int j=0; j<n; j++) {
    if(a.charAt(i+j)!=b.charAt(j)) {
      break;
    }
    else if(j==n-1) {
      return true;
    }
  }
}
return false;
}
```

Listing 3.3: Sub String

3.4.4 Analysis

Time Complexity

The worst-case scenario occurs when a and b are very similar but do not match until the last possible check. In this case, the algorithm performs $O((m-n+1) * n)$ comparisons, where m is the length of a and n is the length of b. Thus, the worst-case time complexity is $O(mn)$.

Space Complexity

The space complexity is $O(1)$, as the algorithm only uses a few extra variables m, n, i, j and does not allocate any additional space proportional to the input size.

3.5 Reverse order of words

3.5.1 Problem

Reverse order of words in a sentence

Example 1:
Input : How are you
Output : you are How

Example 2:
Input : Hello! This is for testing
Output : testing for is This Hello!

3.5.2 Algorithm

1. Reverse the Entire Sentence

   - Start by reversing the entire string. This operation flips the sentence so that the last word comes first, but each word is also reversed.

2. Split the Sentence into Words

   - Split the reversed sentence into individual words. This can be done by using the space character as a delimiter.

3. Reverse Each Word:

- Iterate through the array of words. Reverse each word so that it is correctly oriented.

4. Reassemble the Sentence

- Join the reversed words back into a single string, adding spaces between each word.

3.5.3 Program

```java
/**
 * Reverse the order of words in a sentence
 * @param str
 */
String reverseOrderOfWords(String str) {
    // Reverse entire sentence
    String reverseStr = reverse(str);

    // Reverse each word in the sentence
    String[] reverseWords = reverseStr.split(" ");
    StringBuilder reverseSb = new StringBuilder();
    for(String word:reverseWords){
        reverseSb.append(reverse(word)).append(" ");
    }
    return reverseSb.toString();
}


/**
 * Reverse the string which is between start index to
   end index
 *
 * @param str
 * @param startIndex
 * @param endIndex
 */
String reverse(String str) {
    char[] charArray = str.toCharArray();
    for(int i=0,j=charArray.length-1; i<j; i++,j--) {
        char temp=charArray[i];
        charArray[i]= charArray[j];
        charArray[j]= temp;
    }
    return String.valueOf(charArray);
}
```

Listing 3.4: Reverse order of words

3.5.4 Analysis

Time Complexity

Reversing the Entire Sentence: O(N), where N is the length of the string. Each character is visited once.

Splitting and Reversing Words: The splitting operation is O(N), as it needs to scan through the entire sentence. Reversing each word takes O(M) per word, where M is the length of the word. However, since the total length of all words combined is N, this step is also O(N) overall.

Reassembling the Sentence: This step is O(N) because each character is added once to the final string.

Overall, the time complexity of the algorithm is O(N), where N is the length of the input string.

Space Complexity

Additional Storage for Words: O(N), to store the reversed sentence and the array of words. Output String: O(N), for the final reversed sentence.

The overall space complexity is O(N), accounting for the storage of the intermediate and final results.

3.6 Longest Palindrome

3.6.1 Problem

Given a string str, find the longest palindromic substring in str.

Example 1:
Input : abb
Output : bb

Example 2:
Input : abba
Output : abba

3.6.2 Algorithm

1. Edge Case Handling

   - If the input string is null or empty (after trimming), immediately return an empty string, as there are no palindromes to find.

2. Initialization

   - Start with a default longest palindrome substring, which can initially be the first character of the string, assuming a non-empty string.

3. Iterative Expansion

   - Iterate through the string, treating each character and each pair of adjacent characters as potential centers of palindromes.

     - For each center (or pair of centers), use the helper method palinAroundCentre to expand in both directions (left and right) as long as the characters match and the boundaries of the string are not exceeded.

     - Compare the length of the newly found palindrome with the current longest palindrome. If it's longer, update the longest palindrome.

4. Return the Longest Palindrome

   - After scanning the entire string, return the longest palindromic substring found.

3.6.3 Program

```
1
2 String palinAroundCentre(String str, int i, int j)
3   {
4      boolean flag=false;
5      while(i>=0 && j<=(str.length()-1) && str.charAt(i) ==
   str.charAt(j)) {
6         i--; j++;
7         flag=true;
8      }
9      if(flag) {
10        return str.substring(i+1, j);
11     } else if(i==j){
```

```
12      return str.substring(i, j+1);
13    } else {
14      return str.substring(i+1, j+1);
15    }
16  }
17
18  String findLongestPalindrome(String str)
19  {
20    if(str == null || str.trim().length() == 0)
21      return "";
22    // get the length of string
23    int n = str.length();
24    String longPalin = str.substring(0,1);
25    for(int i=0; i < n-1; i++) {
26
27      String palin = palinAroundCentre(str, i, i);
28      if(palin.length() > longPalin.length()) {
29        longPalin = palin;
30      }
31
32      palin = palinAroundCentre(str, i, i+1);
33      if(palin.length()>longPalin.length()) {
34        longPalin = palin;
35      }
36    }
37    return longPalin;
38  }
```

Listing 3.5: Longest Palindrome

3.6.4 Analysis

Time Complexity

The main part of the algorithm iterates through the string once (O(N)), and for each character, it potentially expands across the length of the string in the worst case (O(N) again). Thus, the overall time complexity is $O(N^2)$, where N is the length of the string.

Space Complexity

The space used by the algorithm is $O(1)$ for variables holding indices, lengths, and the current longest palindrome. The output space for the longest palindrome does not count towards the algorithm's space complexity as it is required for the output.

Chapter 4

Hash Maps

4.1 Introduction

4.1.1 Hash Map

Hash Map is a data structure that stores the data in (Key, Value) pairs but it is un-synchronized. It allows to store the null keys as well, but there should be only one null key object and there can be any number of null values.

```
// Declare a HashMap
HashMap<String, Integer> map = new HashMap<>();
```

4.2 First non repeated character in a string

4.2.1 Problem

Write a program to print first non repeated character in a string.

Example 1:
Input : hello how are you
Output : w

Example 2:
Input : Hi there
Output : H

4.2.2 Algorithm

1. Build a Hash Map with number occurrences of each character in the given string

2. In second pass, check the count of every character. Whenever we hit a count of 1 then that is the first unique character in a given string.

3. None if all characters are repeated in a given string

4.2.3 Program

```java
import java.util.HashMap;

public class  FirstNonRepeatedchar{
    private static final int CHARS = 256;

    private HashMap<Character, Integer> hm = new HashMap<
    Character, Integer>(CHARS);

    /**
     * Build HashMap with count of characters occurances
     */
    void getCharCountArray(String str) {
        for (int i = 0; i < str.length(); i++) {
            // If character already occurred,
            if (hm.containsKey(str.charAt(i))) {
                // increment character count
                hm.put(str.charAt(i), hm.get(str.charAt(i)
    )+1);
            } else {
                //If it's first occurrence then store a
    char and count = 1
                hm.put(str.charAt(i), 1);
            }
        }
    }

    /**
     * Print the first non repreated character
     *
     **/
    void firstNonRepeatedChar(String str) {
        getCharCountArray(str);
        int result = -1;
        for (Character key : str.toCharArray()) {
            int c = hm.get(key);
            if (c == 1 ) {
                System.out.println(key);
                return;
```

```
37              }
38          }
39
40          System.out.println("None");
41      }
42
43      // Driver method
44      public static void main(String[] args) {
45          String str1 = "hello how are you";
46          FirstNonRepeatedchar fnrc = new
        FirstNonRepeatedchar();
47
48          fnrc.firstNonRepeatedChar(str1);
49      }
50 }
```

Listing 4.1: First non repeated character in a string

4.2.4 Analysis

Time Complexity

Populating the HashMap: $O(n)$, where n is the length of the string. Each character is processed once.

Finding the first non-repeating character: $O(n)$ in the worst case, because in the worst scenario, you might need to scan all characters in the string again to find the first non-repeating character based on the counts stored in the HashMap.

Overall, the total time complexity is $O(n) + O(n) = O(n)$, where n is the length of the string.

Space Complexity

The space complexity is mainly due to the HashMap used to store character counts. In the worst case (when all characters are unique), the space complexity is $O(n)$, where n is the length of the string. However, for strings with a limited set of characters (e.g., ASCII characters), the space complexity would be $O(k)$, where k is the number of unique characters in the string, which can be much less than n.

4.3 Check Brackets

4.3.1 Problem

Given a string s containing just the characters '(', ')', '{', '}', '[' and ']', determine if the input string is valid with matching brackets.

An input string is valid if:

- Open brackets must be closed by the same type of brackets.

- Open brackets must be closed in the correct order.

Example 1:
Input : s = "[]"
Output : true

Example 2:
Input : s = "()[]"
Output : true

Example 3:
Input : s = "(]"
Output : false

Example 4:
Input : s = "([)]"
Output : false

4.3.2 Algorithm

1. Initialize a stack to temporarily hold opening brackets.
2. Create a mapping (HashMap) for closing to opening brackets

- ')' -> '('

- '}' -> '{'

- ']' -> '['

3. Iterate over each character in the input string:

- If it's a closing bracket

  - Check if the stack is empty or the top of the stack doesn't match the corresponding opening bracket in the mapping. If so, return false.

  - Otherwise, pop the top element from the stack.

- If it's an opening bracket, push it onto the stack.

4. Return true if the stack is empty, indicating all brackets were properly closed and nested; otherwise, return false.

4.3.3   Program

```
class Brackets {

  // Hash table that takes care of the map.
  private HashMap<Character, Character> map;

  // Initialize hash map with mappings. This simply makes
    the code easier to read.
  public Brackets() {
    this.map = new HashMap<Character, Character>();
    this.map.put(')', '(');
    this.map.put('}', '{');
    this.map.put(']', '[');
  }

  public boolean isValid(String s) {

    // Initialize a stack to be used in the algorithm.
    Stack<Character> stack = new Stack<Character>();

    for (int i = 0; i < s.length(); i++) {
      char c = s.charAt(i);

      // If the current character is a closing bracket.
      if (map.containsKey(c)) {

        // Get the top element of the stack. If the stack
    is empty, set a dummy value '#'
        char topElement = stack.empty() ? '#' : stack.pop
();

        // If the mapping for this bracket doesn't match,
    return false.
        if (topElement != map.get(c)) {
          return false;
```

```
32          }
33      } else {
34          // If it was an opening bracket, push to the stack

35          stack.push(c);
36      }
37  }
38
39  // If the stack still contains elements, then it is an
    invalid expression.
40  return stack.isEmpty();
41  }
42
43  public static void main(String[] args) {
44      String str1 = "{[]}";
45      Brackets b = new Brackets();
46      System.out.println(b.isValid(str1));
47  }
48 }
```

Listing 4.2: Check Brackets

4.3.4 Analysis

Time Complexity: O(n), where n is the length of the input string. The algorithm iterates through each character exactly once.

Space Complexity: O(n) in the worst case, when all characters are opening brackets, necessitating that they all be stored in the stack. For balanced strings or strings with fewer opening brackets, the space used will be less.

Summary

This program efficiently validates bracket correctness with linear time and potentially less-than-linear space usage, making it highly effective for even large strings.

Chapter 5

Recursion

5.1 Introduction

Recursion is a concept or process depends on a simpler or smaller instances of the same problem. For example, finding a factorial of given number, Fibonacci series, Towers of Honoi etc.

5.2 Factorial

5.2.1 Problem

Write a program to find factorial of a given number. For example, 5 factorial is 120 (i.e. 5*4*3*2*1).

Example 1:
Input : 3
Output : 6

Example 2:
Input : 6
Output : 720

5.2.2 Algorithm

1. **Base Case**: If n is less than or equal to 1 (n <= 1), return 1. This condition handles the case for n = 0 and n = 1, both of which have a factorial value of 1.

2. **Recursive Case**: If n is not 1, the function returns n multiplied by the factorial of n-1. This step breaks down the problem into a smaller sub-problem, leveraging the fact that the factorial of n is n times the factorial of n-1.

5.2.3 Program

```
1
2 /**
3  * WAP to find factorial of a given number
4  *
5  */
6 public class Factorial {
7
8    public int fact(int n){
9      if(n<=1) { // Base case
10         return 1;
11     } else {
12         return n * fact(n-1); // Recursive step
13     }
14   }
15
16   /**
17    * @param args
18    */
19   public static void main(String[] args) {
20      // TODO Auto-generated method stub
21      Factorial f = new Factorial();
22       int n=6;
23       for(int i=1; i<=n; i++) {
24          System.out.print(f.fact(i) + " ");
25       }
26
27   }
28
29 }
```

Listing 5.1: Factorial

5.2.4 Analysis

Time Complexity: O(n). Each call to fact reduces the problem size by 1, leading to n calls in total for a number n.

Space Complexity: O(n). Each recursive call adds a layer to the call stack, resulting in n layers for a number n. This is due to the function waiting for the result of the next recursive call before it can return its result.

Summary

This recursive approach is a classic and easy-to-understand method for computing factorials. However, the space complexity can be an issue for very large n due to the depth of the recursion potentially causing a stack overflow. For large values of n, an iterative approach might be more space-efficient, operating with $O(1)$ additional space.

5.3   Fibonacci Series

5.3.1   Problem

Write a program to print Fibonacci Series.

Example 1:
Input : n = 6
Output : 0 1 1 2 3 5

5.3.2   Algorithm

The Fibonacci series is another classic example of recursion:

Base cases:
If n is 1, return 0. This is because the first number in the Fibonacci sequence (0-indexed) is 0.

If n is 2, return 1. This is because the second number in the Fibonacci sequence is 1.

Recursive step:
Fib(n) = Fib(n - 1) + Fib(n - 2) for all integers n > 1.

For n > 2, return the sum of fiboRec(n-1) and fiboRec(n-2). This reflects the Fibonacci sequence's definition, where each number is the sum of the two preceding ones.

5.3.3 Program

```
1
2  /**
3   * WAP to print Fibonacci Series
4   *
5   */
6  public class Fibonacci {
7
8    public int fiboRec(int n){
9      if(n==1){ // Base case 1
10         return 0;
11     } else if(n==2){ // Base case 2
12         return 1;
13     } else {
14         return fiboRec(n-1)+fiboRec(n-2); // Recursive step
15     }
16   }
17
18   /**
19    * @param args
20    */
21   public static void main(String[] args) {
22     // TODO Auto-generated method stub
23     Fibonacci f = new Fibonacci();
24       int n=6;
25       for(int i=1; i<=n; i++) {
26         System.out.print(f.fiboRec(i) + " ");
27       }
28
29   }
30
31 }
```

Listing 5.2: Fibonacci Series

5.3.4 Analysis

Time Complexity: $O(2^n)$. The time complexity is exponential because each function call, fiboRec(n), generates two more calls. This results in a call tree that grows exponentially with the depth of n.

Space Complexity: $O(n)$. The space complexity is linear due to the depth of the recursive call stack. In the worst case, there are n recursive calls on the stack before reaching the base case.

Summary

The recursive approach is straightforward and elegant but not efficient for large n due to its exponential time complexity and the fact that it recalculates values for the same inputs multiple times. To improve efficiency, one could use dynamic programming techniques like memoization or an iterative approach, which both have a polynomial time complexity of O(n).

5.4 Towers of Honoi

5.4.1 Problem

Write a program to solve Towers of Honoi problem.

The objective of the puzzle is to move the entire stack to one of the other rods, obeying the following rules:

There are three rods left, center and right and n disks. All the disks are placed on left rod in order (smallest disk at the top and largest disk at the bottom). We need to move all the disks from left to right to maintain same order with following rules
1. Only one disk need to be moved at a time.
2. Each move consists of taking the upper disk from one of the stacks and placing it on top of another stack or on an empty rod.
3. No disk may be placed on top of a disk that is smaller than it.

5.4.2 Algorithm

1. Move n-1 disks from left to center using right as a temporary
2. Move disk n from left to right
3. Move n-1 disks from center to right using left as a temporary

5.4.3 Program

```
1
2 public class TowersOfHonoi {
3   void Honoi(int n, String left, String right, String
    centre) {
4     if(n>0){
```

```
 5          Honoi(n-1, left, centre, right);
 6          System.out.println(" Move disk " + n + " from " +
        left + " to " + right);
 7          Honoi(n-1, centre, right, left);
 8      }
 9  }
10
11  /**
12   * @param args
13   */
14  public static void main(String[] args) {
15      // TODO Auto-generated method stub
16
17      TowersOfHonoi h = new TowersOfHonoi();
18      h.Honoi(3, "left", "right", "centre");
19  }
20
21 }
```

Listing 5.3: Towers of Honoi

5.4.4 Analysis

Time Complexity: $O(2^n)$. The time complexity is exponential because each invocation of the Honoi function leads to two further invocations, except for the base case. The number of moves required to solve the puzzle is exactly $2^n - 1$.

Space Complexity: $O(n)$. The space complexity is linear due to the maximum height of the call stack, which corresponds to the number of disks n. Each recursive call adds a layer to the call stack until the base case is reached.

Summary

This recursive method elegantly captures the essence of the Tower of Hanoi problem and provides a clear procedure for solving it, regardless of the number of disks involved.

5.5 Power

5.5.1 Problem

Write a program to calculate x to the power of n. For example, 2 to the power of 3 is 8 (i.e. 2*2*2).

Example 1:
Input : 2 4
Output : 16

Example 2:
Input : 5 3
Output : 125

5.5.2 Algorithm

1. Base Cases:

   - If n=0, the function returns 1 since any number raised to the power of 0 is 1.

   - If n=1, it returns x itself, as any number raised to the power of 1 is the number itself.

2. Even Exponent

   - If n is even, the function computes $x^{n/2}$ and then squares it. This is because $x^n = (x^{n/2})^2$. This step reduces the number of multiplications significantly, especially for large n.

3. Odd Exponent

   - If n is odd, the function computes $x^{n/2}$, squares it, and then multiplies by x one more time. This is because $x^n = x \cdot (x^{n/2})^2$.

5.5.3 Program

```
public class Power {

    int power(int x, int n) {
        if(n == 0)
```

```
6        return 1;
7      else if(n == 1)
8        return x;
9      else if(n%2 == 0)
10       return power(x*x, n/2);
11     else
12       return x*power(x*x, n/2);
13   }
14
15   /**
16    * @param args
17    */
18   public static void main(String[] args) {
19      // TODO Auto-generated method stub
20
21      Power p = new Power();
22      int x=2,n=10;
23      System.out.println(x + " to the power of " + n + " is
         "+p.power(x, n));
24
25   }
26 }
```

Listing 5.4: X to the power of n

5.5.4 Analysis

Time Complexity: $O(\log n)$. The algorithm divides the problem size by 2 with each recursive call (for even n), leading to a logarithmic number of steps. This is a significant improvement over the linear complexity of the naive approach.

Space Complexity: $O(\log n)$. The space complexity is determined by the height of the recursion tree, which grows logarithmically with n. Each recursive call adds a layer to the call stack until the base case is reached.

Summary

This implementation of the power function is highly efficient for computing large powers, significantly reducing both the time and space complexities compared to the naive approach. The use of exponentiation by squaring makes it particularly useful in algorithms where large power computations are required.

This method is also a classic example of divide-and-conquer strategy,

breaking down the problem into smaller subproblems, solving each sub-
problem just once, and combining their results efficiently.

5.6   Decimal to Binary

5.6.1   Problem

Write a program to convert Decimal (n>0) to Binary number.

Example 1:
Input : 4
Output : 100

Example 2:
Input : 10
Output : 1010

5.6.2   Algorithm

Base Case: If n is 0, the recursion stops. Since the function doesn't explicitly handle the case when n is 0 (it just doesn't proceed with further
recursion), it's implicitly considered a base case where nothing happens.

Recursive Step: For a given positive integer n, the function:

- First, recursively calls itself with n divided by 2 (n/2). This step
  continues dividing the number by 2 until it reaches 0.

- After reaching the base case, as the recursion unwinds, it prints
  the remainder of n divided by 2 (n%2). This step converts the
  decimal number to binary by collecting the remainders of successive
  divisions by 2, from the least significant bit to the most significant
  bit.

How It Works

For example, to convert the decimal number 10 to binary:

- First call: n = 10, 10/2 = 5, go to the recursive call with n = 5.

- Second call: n = 5, 5/2 = 2, go to the recursive call with n = 2.

- Third call: n = 2, 2/2 = 1, go to the recursive call with n = 1.

- Fourth call: n = 1, 1/2 = 0, base case reached, start unwinding.

- Print 1%2 = 1 (LSB), then back to n = 2, print 2%2 = 0, then n = 5, print 5%2 = 1, and finally n = 10, print 10

The printed sequence is 1010, which is the binary representation of the decimal number 10.

5.6.3 Program

```java
public class DecimalToBinary {

  void decimalToBinary(int n)
  {
    if(n>0) {
      decimalToBinary(n/2);
      System.out.print(n%2);
    }
  }

  public static void main(String[] args) {
    // TODO Auto-generated method stub
    DecimalToBinary db = new DecimalToBinary();
    int n = 10;
    System.out.println("Decimal number : " + n);
    db.decimalToBinary(n);
  }
}
```

Listing 5.5: Decimal to Binary

5.6.4 Analysis

Time Complexity: O(log n). Each recursive call divides n by 2, so the depth of the recursion, and thus the number of divisions (and remainder operations), is proportional to the logarithm of n.

Space Complexity: O(log n). The maximum depth of the call stack is also proportional to the logarithm of n, as the function makes a single recursive call for each division by 2 until n reaches 0.

Summary

This method efficiently leverages the divide-and-conquer strategy, breaking the problem into smaller parts (dividing the number by 2), solving them (calculating the remainder), and combining them in reverse order of execution to form the final binary representation.

5.7 Climb Stairs

5.7.1 Problem

Let's assume that you are climbing a stair case. Each time you can either climb 1 or 2 steps. It will take n steps to reach to the top.

Write a program to calculate how many distinct ways you can climb to the top.

Example 1:
Input : 2
Output : 2

Example 2:
Input : 5
Output : 8

5.7.2 Algorithm

This problem is much similar to Fibonacci problem, one way to do this as below:
1. $F(0) = 1$
2. $F(1) = 1$
2. $F(n) = F(n-1) + F(n-2)$

1. Initialization

- An integer array s of size n+1 is created to store the number of ways to climb to each step i from 0 to n.

2. Base Cases

- If i is less than 0, it means an invalid step, so return 0.

- If i is 0, it means standing on the ground floor, and there's exactly 1 way to be at step 0 (not climbing any steps).

3. Memoization

- Before computing the number of ways to climb to step i, check if s[i] already has a non-zero value (indicating the result has already been computed). If so, return s[i].

4. Recursive Calculation

- If s[i] is not yet calculated, it is set to the sum of the number of ways to climb to step i-1 and step i-2. This captures the idea that to reach step i, one could have taken a single step from i-1 or a double step from i-2.

5. Return Value

- The function cs returns the value of s[i], which represents the total number of ways to climb to step i.

5.7.3 Program

```java
public int climbStairs(int n) {
    int[] s = new int[n+1];
    return cs(s, n);
}
public int cs(int[] s, int i){
    if(i<0)
        return 0;
    else
    if(i==0)
        return 1;
    if(s[i]!=0) {
        return s[i]; //remove unnessary calculation
    }
    s[i] = cs(s, i-1) + cs(s, i-2);
    return s[i];
}
```

Listing 5.6: Climb Stairs

5.7.4 Analysis

Time Complexity

The time complexity of the algorithm is O(n). This efficiency is achieved by avoiding the re-computation of the number of ways to reach the same step, thanks to memoization. Each step from 1 to n is computed exactly once and stored for future reference.

Space Complexity

The space complexity is also O(n) due to the storage requirements of the memoization array s. This array is used to store the computed number of ways to reach each step up to n.

Summmary

This dynamic programming approach with memoization is a highly efficient solution for the Climbing Stairs problem. It ensures that each subproblem is solved only once and uses the results of these subproblems to construct the solution to the original problem, significantly reducing the computation time and making it scalable for large values of n.

5.8 Permutations

5.8.1 Problem

Write a program a print all the permissions for a given string. For example, permutations for a string ab are ab and ba.

Example 1:
Input : abcd
Output :
abcd
abdc
acbd
acdb
adbc
adcb
bacd
badc

bcad
bcda
bdac
bdca
cabd
cadb
cbad
cbda
cdab
cdba
dabc
dacb
dbac
dbca
dcab
dcba

5.8.2 Algorithm

Use recursion and indexes effectively to solve this problem

1. Initialization

   - in[]: An input array containing the characters to be permuted.

   - out[]: An output array to store one permutation at a time.

   - used[]: A boolean-like array (using char for flags) to keep track of which characters from the in[] array have been used in the current permutation.

   - size: The total number of characters in the input array, also the size of the in[] and used[] arrays.

   - recLen: The current length of the permutation being constructed in out[]. Initially, this is 0.

2. Base Case

   - When recLen equals size, it means a complete permutation of length size has been constructed in out[]. This permutation is printed, and the function returns to explore other permutations.

3. Recursive Case

- Iterate through each character in in[]:

  - If a character is already used in the current permutation (used[i] == 1), skip it.

  - Otherwise, place the current character in[i] in the output array at the position recLen, mark it as used (used[i] = 1), and call Permute recursively with recLen + 1 to construct the next character of the permutation.

  - After returning from the recursive call, backtrack by marking the character as unused (used[i] = 0) to explore other permutations that include this character in different positions.

5.8.3 Program

```
 1
 2 public class Permutations {
 3
 4    /**
 5     * Permutations of given string
 6     *
 7     * @param in
 8     * @param out
 9     * @param used
10     * @param size
11     * @param recLen
12     */
13    void Permute(char[] in, char[] out, char[] used, int
       size, int recLen) {
14      if(recLen == size) {
15        System.out.println(String.valueOf(out));
16        return;
17      }
18      for(int i=0; i<size; i++) {
19        if(used[i]==1) {
20          continue;
21        }
22        out[recLen]=in[i];
23        used[i]=1;
24        Permute(in, out, used, size, recLen+1);
25        used[i]=0;
26      }
27    }
28
29    public static void main(String[] args) {
30      // TODO Auto-generated method stub
31
32      Permutations p = new Permutations();
33      String in = "abcd";
```

```
34      int len = in.length();
35      char[] out = new char[len];
36      char[] used = new char[len];
37      System.out.println("Permutations:");
38      p.Permute(in.toCharArray(), out, used, len, 0);
39    }
40
41 }
```

Listing 5.7: Permutations

5.8.4 Analysis

Time Complexity: O(n!), where n is the number of characters to permute. This is because generating all permutations of n characters involves n choices for the first position, (n-1) for the second, continuing down to 1 choice for the last position, leading to n! permutations.

Space Complexity: O(n) for the recursion stack, as the depth of the recursive call stack can go up to n. Additionally, O(n) space for the out[] and used[] arrays each, leading to a total auxiliary space complexity of O(n), disregarding the input size.

Summary

This approach exhaustively generates all possible permutations by systematically considering every character for every position in the output array, ensuring that each permutation is unique through the use of the used[] array.

5.9 Partition to two subsets

5.9.1 Problem

Write a program to determine whether a given set can be partitioned into two subsets such that the sum of elements in both subsets is same.

Example 1:
Input : a = 1, 5, 11, 5
Output : true
The array can be partitioned two equal sum subsets as 1, 5, 5 and 11

Example 2:
Input : a = 1, 5, 3
Output : false
The array can't be partitioned into two equal sum subsets.

5.9.2   Algorithm

1. Calculate sum of the array. If sum is odd, there cannot be two subsets with equal sum, so return false.
2. If sum of array elements is even, calculate sum/2 and find a subset of array with sum equal to sum/2.

subSetSum

1.1 Base Conditions

- If sum is 0, a subset with the desired sum has been found, return true.

- If n is 0 and sum is not 0, it's not possible to form the desired sum, return false.

1.2 Recursion

- If the current element is greater than the remaining sum, it cannot be part of a subset that adds up to sum, so exclude it and move to the next element.

- Otherwise, explore both possibilities: excluding or including the current element, and proceed with the recursive calls.

partitionTwoSubsets

- Calculate the total sum of the array elements.

- If the total sum is odd, it's impossible to split the array into two subsets with equal sums, so return false.

- If the total sum is even, use subSetSum to check if a subset with sum equal to half of the total sum exists. If it does, the array can be partitioned as required, so return true.

5.9.3 Program

```java
public class Partition {

  boolean subSetSum(int[] a, int n, int sum) {
    if(sum == 0) {
      return true;
    }
    if(n == 0 && sum != 0) {
      return false;
    }
    if(a[n-1] > sum) {
      return subSetSum(a, n-1, sum);
    }
    return subSetSum(a, n-1, sum) || subSetSum(a, n-1, sum
      - a[n-1]);
  }

  boolean partitionTwoSubsets(int[] a) {
    // Calculate sum of the array
    int totalSum = 0;
    for(int i=0; i<a.length; i++) {
      totalSum += a[i];
    }
      // Cann't be divided into two subsets if sum is
    odd
    if(totalSum % 2 != 0) {
      return false;
    }
    else {
        // solve sub-problem recusively if sum is even
      return subSetSum(a, a.length-1, totalSum/2);
    }
  }

  public static void main(String[] args) {
    // TODO Auto-generated method stub
    int a[] = {1, 5, 11, 5};
    Partition p = new Partition();
    System.out.println(p.partitionTwoSubsets(a));
  }
}
```

Listing 5.8: Partition to two subsets

5.9.4 Analysis

Time Complexity: $O(2^n)$, where n is the number of elements in the array. This complexity arises because the algorithm explores two branches (including or excluding an element) for each of the n elements.

Space Complexity: $O(n)$, due to the recursion stack. The maximum depth of the recursive call stack is n, which occurs when the function explores all elements in the array.

Summary

This program is correct but not efficient for large inputs due to its exponential time complexity. For larger inputs, a dynamic programming approach, specifically using the 0/1 knapsack problem solution or bottom-up tabulation, can significantly reduce the time complexity to $O(n*sum)$ where sum is the total sum of the array elements divided by 2. This approach would have a polynomial time complexity, making it more feasible for larger inputs.

Chapter 6

Linked Lists

6.1 Introduction

Linked list is a linear data structure, each node contains an element and a pointer to next node. The elements in the linked list is not stored in a contiguous location.

6.1.1 Advantages

Here are few advantages Linked Lists as compared to Arrays:

- Dynamic size

- Ease and faster insertion and deletion

- Efficient use of memory

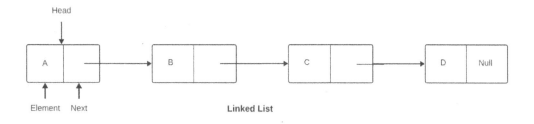

Figure 6.1: Linked List

6.1.2   Definition of List Node

6.1.3   Program

```java
public class ListNode {

  public Integer element;
  public ListNode next;

  /**
   * Constructor with element
   *
   * @param element
   */
  public ListNode(Integer element) {
    this.element = element;
    this.next = null;
  }

  /**
   * Constructor with element and next pointer
   *
   * @param element
   * @param next
   */
  public ListNode(Integer element, ListNode next) {
    this.element = element;
    this.next = next;
  }
}
```

Listing 6.1: Definition of List Node

6.2   Print Singly Linked List

6.2.1   Problem

Write a program to print values of singly linked list.

Example 1:
Input : 1 –> 2 –> 3 –> 4
Output : The linked list : 1–>2–>3–>4

6.2.2 Algorithm

1. Check Empty List: If header.next is null, print "Empty list" and exit.
2. Print Header: Output "The linked list :" to indicate the start of the list elements.
3. Traverse and Print: For each node p starting from header.next:
   - 3.1 Print p.element.
   - 3.2 If p.next is not null, print "->"; else, continue.
4. End Output: Print a newline character after the last element.

6.2.3 Program

```
1   public void printList() {
2       // Assuming ListNode is a class with fields 'element'
        for data and 'next' for the link to the next node.
3       if (header.next == null) {
4           System.out.println("Empty list");
5           return;
6       }
7       System.out.print("The linked list : ");
8       for (ListNode p = header.next; p != null; p = p.next)
        {
9           System.out.print(p.element + (p.next != null ? "
        -->" : ""));
10      }
11      System.out.println();
12  }
```

Listing 6.2: Print Singly Linked List

6.2.4 Analysis

Time Complexity

The time complexity of the printList() method is $O(n)$, where n is the number of elements in the linked list. This is because the method iterates through each element of the list exactly once to print it.

Space Complexity

The space complexity of the method is $O(1)$. The method uses a fixed amount of extra space (a few variables, notably the p pointer) regardless of the size of the input list. The space used for output to the console is not typically counted towards space complexity in algorithm analysis.

Efficiency and Scalability

The algorithm is efficient for its purpose, as it traverses the list only once to print all elements. This is the best possible time complexity for this task since every element must be examined.
The method is scalable in terms of the number of elements in the list. The time to complete the operation grows linearly with the number of elements, which is expected for operations on a linked list.

Maintainability and Readability

The use of a single loop and conditional (ternary) operator for printing makes the method concise and easy to understand. The early return for an empty list improves readability by reducing the nesting level and clarifying the method's behavior in edge cases.

In conclusion, the printList() method provides a straightforward, efficient way to print the elements of a linked list, adhering to good coding practices for clarity, efficiency, and maintainability.

6.3   Insert a Node

6.3.1   Problem

Write a program to insert a new node with value x after a node p

Example 1:
Input : a -> b -> p -> z
Output : a -> b -> p -> x -> z

6.3.2   Algorithm

1. Check for Valid p Node:
   .   Verify if the node p provided as the insertion point is not null.
   .   If p is null, do nothing and exit the method. This prevents attempts to insert after an undefined (non-existent) node.

2. Insert New Node After p:
   .   Create a new node with the value x.
   .   Set the new node's next field to p.next, linking it to the subsequent part of the list.

. Update p.next to point to the new node, effectively inserting it into the list.

6.3.3 Program

```java
/**
 * Insert a node after p node in linked list
 * @param p
 * @param x
 */
public void insert(ListNode p, Integer x)
{
    if (p != null) {
            p.next = new ListNode(x, p.next);
        }
}
```

Listing 6.3: Insert a node

6.3.4 Analysis

Time Complexity: O(1)

The insertion operation consists of a few constant-time statements, including creating a new node and updating pointers. There are no loops or recursive calls that depend on the size of the list, making the time complexity constant.

Space Complexity: O(1)

The method creates a single new ListNode regardless of the input list's size, resulting in constant space usage. No additional data structures or recursive stack space are involved.

Key Points

Efficiency: The method is highly efficient, with both time and space complexities being O(1). This makes it suitable for frequent insertions in a linked list.

Robustness: The preliminary null check for p ensures that the method does not attempt to operate on an invalid (null) reference, which would otherwise result in a NullPointerException.

Simplicity: The algorithm is straightforward, focusing solely on the task of insertion without unnecessary complications, enhancing readability and maintainability.

In conclusion, the insert method provides an optimal and straightforward approach for inserting a new node into a linked list at a specific position, with excellent performance characteristics.

6.4   Reverse Linked List

6.4.1   Problem

Write a program to reverse a singly linked list.

Example 1:
Input : 1 -> 2 -> 3 -> 4 -> 5
Output : 5 -> 4 -> 3 -> 2 -> 1

Algorithm

The provided method `reverse(ListNode header)` reverses the linked list that starts from the `header.next`. Here is a step-by-step breakdown of the algorithm:

1. Initialize Pointers

- `prevNode` is set to `null`. This will be used to reverse the direction of the links.

- `currNode` starts at `header.next`, the first actual element in the list.

- `nextNode` is used to temporarily store the next node in the list.

2. Traverse the List

- Loop until `currNode` is `null`, indicating the end of the list has been reached.

- Inside the loop, perform the following steps:

  - Store the next node (`currNode.next`) in `nextNode` to maintain the list's traversal.

- Reverse the link by setting `currNode.next` to `prevNode`.
- Move `prevNode` forward to the current node (`currNode`).
- Proceed to the next node in the original list by setting `currNode` to `nextNode`.

3. Update Header

- After the loop, set `header.next` to `prevNode`, which now points to the new first node of the reversed list.

6.4.2 Program

```
/**
 * Reverse the linked list
 *
 */
public void reverse(ListNode header) {
        ListNode prevNode, currNode, nextNode;
        prevNode = null;
        currNode = header.next;
        while(currNode != null) {
                nextNode = currNode.next;
                currNode.next = prevNode;
                prevNode = currNode;
                currNode = nextNode;
        }
        header.next = prevNode;
}
```

Listing 6.4: Reverse Linked List

6.4.3 Analysis

Time Complexity: O(n)
The time complexity is linear (O(n)), where n is the number of nodes in the list. This is because the algorithm iterates through the list exactly once, performing a constant amount of work for each node (reversing pointers).

Space Complexity: O(1)
The space complexity is constant because the algorithm uses a fixed number of pointers (variables) regardless of the input list's size. It modifies the list in place without requiring additional space proportional to the list's size.

Key Points

In-Place Reversal: The algorithm reverses the list in place, meaning it does not create a new list but instead changes the pointers in the existing list.

Efficient: Given the constraints of singly linked list data structures, the method is as efficient as possible in both time and space.

Robustness: The method correctly handles the edge case of an empty list (when `header.next` is `null`) by effectively doing nothing, which is the expected behavior.

In summary, this `reverse` method provides a straightforward and efficient way to reverse a singly linked list in place, with optimal time and space complexity characteristics.

6.5 Reverse k nodes

6.5.1 Problem

Write a program to reverse every k nodes in a given singly linked list

Example 1:
Input : 1 −> 2 −> 3 −> 4, k=2
Output : 2 −> 1 −> 4 −> 3

Example 2:
Input : 1 −> 2 −> 3, k=2
Output : 2 −> 1 −> 3

6.5.2 Algorithm

1. Base Condition

- Check if the head (h) of the list is null. If it is, return null, as there are no nodes to reverse.

2. Initialization

- Initialize three pointers: current to h (the start of the block to be reversed), prev to null (to reverse the links), and next to null (to temporarily store the next node).

3. Reverse k Nodes

- Loop up to k times or until current becomes null (end of list reached):
    - Temporarily store the next node (current.next) in next.
    - Reverse the current node's pointer to point to prev.
    - Move prev forward to current.
    - Move current forward to next.
    - Increment the counter count.

4. Recursive Call for Remaining Blocks

- If next is not null after the loop, it means there are more nodes left to process. Make a recursive call with next as the new head and k as the block size. Set the result of this call as the next of the last node of the reversed block (h.next).

5. Return New Head:

- Return prev as the new head of the reversed block. This is because, after the reversal, prev points to the first node of the reversed block.

6.5.3 Program

```
/**
 * Reverse every k nodes in a given linked list
 * example: i/p: 1->2->3->4    o/p:2->1->4->3
 *
 * @param l
 * @param k
 * @return
 */
public ListNode ReverseBlock(ListNode h, int k) {
    if(h==null) {
        return null;
    }
    else {
        int count=0;
        ListNode current, prev, next;
```

```
17    current=h;
18    prev=next=null;
19    while(current!=null && count<k){
20       next = current.next;
21       current.next = prev;
22       prev=current;
23       current=next;
24       count++;
25    }
26    // reverse remaining block of nodes
27    if(next!=null) {
28       h.next = ReverseBlock(next, k);
29    }
30    // return new header node
31    return prev;
32    }
33 }
```

Listing 6.5: Reverse k nodes

6.5.4 Analysis

Time Complexity: $O(n)$

The algorithm iterates through each node exactly once. Despite the recursive calls, each node is processed once for reversal, leading to a linear time complexity.

Space Complexity: $O(n/k)$

The recursive calls add overhead to the call stack, with the depth of the recursion depending on the number of blocks (n/k), where n is the total number of nodes. Thus, the space complexity is proportional to the number of recursive calls.

Key Insights

In-Place Reversal: The method reverses each block in place, altering the pointers without using additional lists or arrays.

Recursive Connection: After reversing a block, the method recursively handles the rest of the list, ensuring that the end of the reversed block is correctly connected to the start of the next reversed block.

Edge Cases: The algorithm gracefully handles cases where the number of nodes is not a multiple of k by reversing the last set of nodes (less than k) as they are.

This method efficiently achieves the task of reversing every k nodes in a linked list, ensuring proper connection between the reversed blocks and handling various edge cases gracefully.

6.6 Merge Sorted Linked Lists

6.6.1 Problem

Write a program to merge two sorted singly linked lists

Example 1:
Input : L1 : 1 -> 2 -> 3 -> 4, L2 : 1 -> 3 -> 5
Output : 1 -> 1 -> 2 -> 3 -> 3 -> 4 -> 5

Example 2:
Input : L1 : 1 -> 5, L2 : 2 -> 3 -> 4
Output : 1 -> 2 -> 3 -> 4 -> 5

6.6.2 Algorithm

1. Handle Base Cases

   - If l1 is null, return l2 directly as the merged list.

   - If l2 is null, return l1 as the merged list.

2. Initialize the Merged List (l3)

   - Compare the first elements of l1 and l2.

   - Initialize l3 to the list with the smaller first element. This will be the head of the merged list.

   - Advance l3 to its next node (l1 or l2 is updated accordingly).

3. Merge the Lists

   - Iterate while both l1 and l2 have elements.

   - Compare the current elements of l1 and l2.

- Append the smaller element to l3 and advance l3.

- Advance l1 or l2 accordingly (whichever had the smaller element).

4. Append Remaining Elements

- After the loop, one list may have remaining elements while the other is exhausted.

- Directly append the non-empty list to l3 since it's already sorted.

5. Return the Head of the Merged List

- Return the initial node pointed by start, which is the head of the merged sorted list.

6.6.3 Program

```
/**
 * Merge two sorted linked lists
 *
 * @param l1
 * @param l2
 * @return
 */
public static ListNode Merge(ListNode l1, ListNode l2) {
    if(l1==null){
        return l2;
    }
    else if(l2==null){
        return l1;
    }
    else {
    ListNode l3;
        if(l1.element<l2.element){
            l3=l1;
            l1=l1.next;
        }
        else {
            l3=l2;
            l2=l2.next;
        }
        ListNode start = l3;
        while(l1!=null && l2!=null) {
            if(l1.element<l2.element) {
                l3.next=l1;
```

```
30          l1=l1.next;
31        }
32        else {
33           l3.next=l2;
34           l2=l2.next;
35        }
36        l3=l3.next;
37      }
38      if(l1!=null) {
39         l3.next=l1;
40      }
41      if(l2!=null) {
42         l3.next=l2;
43      }
44      return start;
45    }
46  }
```

Listing 6.6: Merge Sorted Linked Lists

6.6.4 Analysis

Time Complexity: O(n + m)

Where n is the length of list l1 and m is the length of list l2. Each list is traversed at most once, making the time complexity linear with respect to the total number of elements in both lists.

Space Complexity: O(1)

The merge operation is performed in place with a few pointers (l3, start), requiring constant extra space.
Note: The method does not create new nodes; it reuses the nodes of the input lists.

Key Points

In-Place and Efficient: The algorithm efficiently merges two sorted lists without needing additional space for nodes.

Stable Merge: The relative order of equal elements from the original lists is preserved in the merged list.

Simplicity: The method uses straightforward comparisons and pointer updates, making it easy to understand and implement.

In summary, this Merge method provides an efficient and space-conserving way to merge two sorted linked lists into a single sorted list, maintaining the order of elements and ensuring stability.

6.7 Swap Adjacent Nodes

6.7.1 Problem

Write a program to swap adjacent nodes in a singly linked list.

Example 1:
Input : 1 –> 2 –> 3 –> 4 –> 5
Output : 2 –> 1 –> 4 –> 3 –> 5

Example 2:
Input : 1 –> 2 –> 3 –> 4
Output : 2 –> 1 –> 4 –> 3

6.7.2 Algorithm

1. Handle Base Cases

- If the list is empty (l == null), return null.

- If the list has only one node (l.next == null), return the list as is, because there's nothing to swap.

2. Initialization

- Initialize p to point to the first node of the list (l). This pointer will be used to traverse the list.

- Set start to the second node (l.next), which will become the new head of the list after the adjacent nodes are swapped.

- Initialize prev to null. This pointer will keep track of the node preceding p to adjust pointers after swaps.

3. Swap Adjacent Nodes

- Iterate through the list while p and p.next are not null to ensure there are at least two nodes to swap.

- Temporarily store p.next in temp, which is the node to be swapped with p.

- Adjust p's next pointer to temp.next, effectively removing temp from its current position.

- Set temp.next to p, swapping p and temp.

- If prev is not null, link prev.next to temp to maintain the list's integrity.

- Update prev to p for the next iteration.

- Move p forward to p.next (the next pair's first node).

4. Return New Head

- Return start, which is the head of the modified list after swapping adjacent nodes.

6.7.3 Program

```
public ListNode SwapAdjacentNodes(ListNode l){
if(l==null)
    return null;
else if(l.next == null)
    return l;
else {
    ListNode p=l;
    ListNode start=l.next;
    ListNode prev=null;
    while(p!=null && p.next!=null){
        ListNode temp=p.next;
        p.next=temp.next;
        temp.next=p;
        if(prev!=null){
            prev.next=temp;
        }
        prev=p;
        p=p.next;
    }
    return start;
}
}
```

Listing 6.7: Swap Adjacent Nodes

6.7.4 Analysis

Time Complexity: O(n)

The method iterates through the list once, with n being the total number of nodes in the list. Each step involves a constant amount of work (swapping pointers), so the overall time complexity is linear.

Space Complexity: O(1)

The space complexity is constant because the algorithm only uses a fixed number of pointers (p, start, prev, temp) regardless of the input size. It modifies the list in place without allocating any additional nodes or data structures.

Key Insights

In-Place Modification: The algorithm swaps nodes in place, altering their next pointers without creating new nodes, thus conserving memory.

Handles Edge Cases: It gracefully handles lists with odd numbers of nodes by leaving the last node in its original position when there's no adjacent node to swap with.

New Head: The method correctly identifies and returns the new head of the list after swaps, which is essential when the original list's head changes as a result of the swapping.

This method offers a straightforward and efficient solution to swap adjacent nodes in a linked list, ensuring the list's structural integrity while managing various list sizes and configurations.

6.8 Middle of Linked List

6.8.1 Problem

Write a program to find middle node of a single linked list by traversing the list only one.
Example 1:
Input : 1 -> 2 -> 3 -> 4 -> 5
Output : 3

Example 2:

Input : 1 -> 2 -> 3 -> 4
Output : 3

6.8.2 Algorithm

1. Initialization

   - Initialize two pointers, slow and fast, both pointing to the header of the list. The header is assumed to be a dummy node at the start of the list, or the actual first node if the list does not use a dummy header.

2. Traversal:

   - While fast and its next node fast.next are not null, perform the following steps:

     – Move slow one step forward (slow = slow.next).

     – Move fast two steps forward (fast = fast.next.next).

   - This loop continues until fast reaches the end of the list or becomes null (in case of an even number of elements, when fast tries to move beyond the last element).

3. Middle Node

   - When the loop terminates, slow will be at the middle of the list. For lists with an odd number of elements, slow will be exactly at the middle. For lists with an even number of elements, slow will be at the start of the second half of the list (which is one of the two "middle" positions, the other being slow.next).

4. Return Middle Node

   - The method returns the slow pointer, which now points to the middle node of the list.

6.8.3 Program

```
1
2   public ListNode findMiddle(ListNode header) {
3     ListNode slow=header, fast=header;
4     while(fast != null && fast.next != null) {
5       slow = slow.next;
6           fast = fast.next.next;
7     }
8     return slow;
9   }
```

Listing 6.8: Middle of Linked List

6.8.4 Analysis

Time Complexity: $O(n)$

The algorithm's time complexity is $O(n)$ where n is the number of nodes in the list. This is because, in the worst case, the fast pointer traverses the entire list, moving two steps at a time, while the slow pointer moves one step at a time. Essentially, the loop's iteration count is proportional to the number of elements in the list divided by two.

Space Complexity: $O(1)$

The space complexity is constant, $O(1)$, because the algorithm uses only two pointers (slow and fast) regardless of the input list size. No additional structures or recursive stack space are used, making this method space-efficient.

Key Insights

Efficiency: The two-pointer technique allows the method to find the middle node in a single pass through the list, which is more efficient than, for example, first counting the list's length and then traversing to the middle.

Even/Odd Length Handling: For lists with an even number of nodes, the method returns the first node of the second half as the "middle." This behavior is a common convention, but specific applications may require adjustment.

Applicability: This method is widely applicable in problems requiring list manipulation, such as reversing the second half of the list, cycle detection, or merging two lists.

In summary, the findMiddle method provides an efficient and straight-forward approach to locating the middle node of a linked list, utilizing the fast and slow pointer technique to achieve optimal time and space complexity.

6.9   Find Nth Node from end

6.9.1   Problem

Write a program to find nth node from end of singly linked list (n>0).
Example 1:
Input : 1->2->3->4->5, and n = 2
Output : 4

Example 2:
Input : 1->2->3->4->5, and n = 1
Output : 5

6.9.2   Algorithm

1. Create a Dummy Node

   - A dummy node is created and pointed to the head of the list. This simplifies edge cases, particularly when removing the first real node of the list.

2. Advance current Pointer

   - The current pointer, initially at the dummy node, is advanced n + 1 times. This positions it right after the target node for removal, ensuring there's a gap of n nodes between current and behind.

3. Advance current and behind Together:

   - Both current and behind pointers are moved forward until current reaches the end of the list. At this point, behind is exactly before the node to be removed.

4. Remove the Node

   - The node after behind is skipped over by adjusting behind.next to behind.next.next, effectively removing the nth node from the end.

5. Return the Modified List

- The method returns dummy.next, which points to the head of the modified list.

6.9.3   Program

```
ListNode removeNthFromEnd(ListNode head, int n) {
    ListNode dummy = new ListNode(0); // Dummy node to
    simplify edge cases
    dummy.next = head;
    ListNode current = dummy, behind = dummy;

    // Advance current n + 1 times to position it right
    after the target for removal
    for (int i = 0; i <= n; i++) {
        current = current.next;
    }

    // Move both pointers until current reaches the end
    while (current != null) {
        behind = behind.next;
        current = current.next;
    }

    // Skip the n-th node from the end
    behind.next = behind.next.next;

    return dummy.next; // Return head of the modified list
}
```

Listing 6.9: Find Nth Node from end

6.9.4   Analysis

Time Complexity: O(L), where L is the total number of nodes in the list. The list is traversed twice: first, to advance the current pointer n + 1 times, and second, to move current and behind together until the end of the list. However, these operations are sequential and do not depend on n, making the overall time complexity linear in the size of the list.

Space Complexity: O(1), as the space used by the algorithm does not scale with the size of the input list. Only a fixed number of pointers and a dummy node are used regardless of the list size.

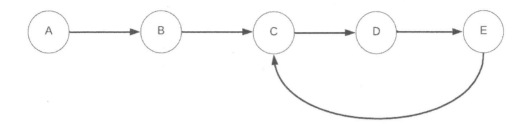

Figure 6.2: Loop in Linked List

Key Insights

Use of Dummy Node: The dummy node simplifies handling the edge case where the head of the list needs to be removed. Without a dummy node, additional conditional checks would be required to handle this case.

Two Pointer Technique: This approach elegantly solves the problem by maintaining a gap of n nodes between two pointers to find the nth node from the end in a single pass through the list (after the initial setup pass).

Edge Case Handling: The method effectively handles all possible values of n, including removing the head of the list, by using the dummy node as a starting point.

This algorithm is efficient and elegant, leveraging the two-pointer technique to avoid having to compute the length of the list explicitly or making multiple passes to identify the node to be removed.

6.10 Detect Loop in Linked List

6.10.1 Problem

Write a program to detect a loop in singly linked list if any.

We can use Floyd's Tortoise and Hare algorithm, which is used to detect cycles (loops) in a linked list. The algorithm uses two pointers, slow and fast, that move at different speeds through the list. Here's a step-by-step breakdown of how the algorithm works and its analysis:

6.10.2 Algorithm

1. Initialization

   - Both slow and fast pointers are initialized to the header of the linked list.

2. Traversal

   - The algorithm enters a loop where slow moves one step at a time (slow = slow.next) and fast moves two steps at a time (fast = fast.next.next). This loop continues as long as slow, fast, and fast.next are not null.

3. Cycle Detection

   - If there is a cycle in the list, the fast pointer, which moves faster, will eventually "lap" the slow pointer, causing both pointers to meet at some node within the cycle. When slow == fast, the method returns true, indicating a loop is detected.

4. Termination

   - If the fast pointer reaches the end of the list (fast == null || fast.next == null), the loop terminates, and the method returns false, indicating that no cycle is present in the list.

6.10.3 Program

```java
public boolean detectLoop(ListNode header) {
    ListNode slow=header, fast=header;
    while(slow != null && fast != null && fast.next !=
    null) {
        slow = slow.next;
        fast = fast.next.next;
        if(slow == fast) {
            return true;
        }
    }
    return false;
}
```

Listing 6.10: Detect Loop in Linked List

6.10.4 Analysis

Time Complexity: $O(N + K)$, where N is the number of nodes outside the loop, and K is the number of nodes in the loop. In the worst case, the time complexity is $O(N)$ for a list with N nodes. This happens because the fast pointer can take at most $N/2$ steps to enter the loop and then at most K steps to meet the slow pointer, where K is less than or equal to N.

Space Complexity: $O(1)$, as the algorithm only uses two pointers regardless of the size of the input list. The space used does not scale with the size of the input.

Key Insights

Efficiency: Floyd's Tortoise and Hare algorithm is an efficient way to detect cycles in a linked list without requiring additional data structures like hash tables, which would increase the space complexity.

Use Cases: Cycle detection is a crucial operation in many applications, including garbage collection algorithms and resource allocation systems, where detecting circular dependencies or deadlocks is necessary.

In Summary, this is a classic example of using two pointers at different speeds to solve a problem efficiently, demonstrating both creativity and mathematical insight into the structure of linked lists.

6.11 Remove Nth Node from end

6.11.1 Problem

Write a program to remove nth node from end of singly linked list (n>0).
Example 1:
Input : 1->2->3->4->5, and n = 2
Output : 1->2->3->5

Example 2:
Input : 1->2->3->4->5, and n = 1
Output : 1->2->3->4

6.11.2 Algorithm

1. Initialize

   - Create a dummy node and point its next to the head of the list. This dummy node serves to simplify edge cases, such as when the head of the list is the node to be removed. Initialize two pointers, current and behind, both pointing to this dummy node.

2. Advance current Pointer

   - Move the current pointer forward n + 1 times. This step positions the current pointer such that there is a gap of n nodes between current and behind, ensuring that when current reaches the end of the list, behind will be just before the node that needs to be removed.

3. Move to the Target Node

   - Continue moving both current and behind forward, one node at a time, until current reaches the end of the list (null). At this point, behind points to the node just before the one that needs to be removed.

4. Remove the Target Node

   - Adjust the next pointer of the node just before the target node (behind) to skip the target node, effectively removing it from the list.

5. Return the New Head

   - Return dummy.next, which points to the head of the modified list.

6.11.3 Program

```java
public ListNode removeNthFromEnd(ListNode head, int n) {
    ListNode dummy = new ListNode(0); // Create a dummy
    node to simplify edge cases
    dummy.next = head;
    ListNode current = dummy, behind = dummy;

```

```
7    // Advance current n + 1 times to position it right
     after the target for removal
8    for (int i = 0; i <= n; i++) {
9        current = current.next;
10   }
11
12   // Move both pointers until current reaches the end
13   while (current != null) {
14       behind = behind.next;
15       current = current.next;
16   }
17
18   // Skip the n-th node from the end
19   behind.next = behind.next.next;
20
21   return dummy.next; // Return head of the modified list
22 }
```

Listing 6.11: Remove Nth Node from end

6.11.4 Analysis

Time Complexity: O(L), where L is the length of the list. The algorithm traverses the list at most twice (first to position current and then to find the nth node from the end), which is still linear.

Space Complexity: O(1). Only a constant amount of extra space is used regardless of the input list size, for the dummy node and pointers.

In Summary, this approach efficiently addresses the problem with optimal space usage, making it effective for singly linked list manipulations.

6.12 Merge Point of Two Linked Lists

6.12.1 Problem

Write a program to find merging point of two linked list.

6.12.2 Algorithm

1. Initialize

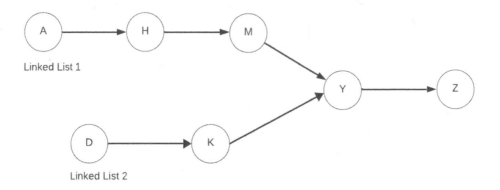

Figure 6.3: Merge point of two linked lists

- Two pointers, curr1 and curr2, are set to the start of header1 and header2 respectively. Two counters, count1 and count2, are used to track the lengths of these lists.

2. Calculate List Lengths

- Traverse each list from start to end to determine their lengths.

3. Equalize Starting Points

- Adjust either curr1 or curr2 to ensure they are the same distance from the merge point. This is achieved by advancing the pointer in the longer list by the difference in lengths.

4. Traversal to Find Merge Point

- Simultaneously advance both pointers through the lists. If they meet (point to the same node), that node is the merge point.

5. Return Merge Point or Null:

- The first node where curr1 and curr2 coincide is returned as the merge point. If no such point is found (the lists do not merge), return null.

6.12.3 Program

```
ListNode findMerge(ListNode header1, ListNode header2) {
    ListNode curr1 = header1, curr2 = header2;
    int count1 = 0, count2 = 0;
    // Calculate lengths of both lists
    while (curr1 != null) {
        count1++;
        curr1 = curr1.next;
    }
    while (curr2 != null) {
        count2++;
        curr2 = curr2.next;
    }
    // Reset pointers to start of their lists
    curr1 = header1;
    curr2 = header2;
    // Align the pointers
    if (count1 > count2) {
        for (int i = 0; i < count1 - count2; i++) curr1 =
    curr1.next;
    } else {
        for (int i = 0; i < count2 - count1; i++) curr2 =
    curr2.next;
    }
    // Find the merge point
    while (curr1 != null && curr2 != null) {
        if (curr1 == curr2) return curr1;
        curr1 = curr1.next;
        curr2 = curr2.next;
    }
    return null;
}
```

Listing 6.12: Merge point of two linked list

6.12.4 Analysis

Time Complexity: The algorithm's time complexity is O(m+n), where m and n are the lengths of the two lists. This includes the time to traverse each list to calculate its length and the time to find the merge point.

Space Complexity: The space complexity is O(1) since only a fixed number of pointers and counters are used, which does not scale with the input size.

In Summary, this function efficiently finds the merge point (if any) between two singly linked lists. It first determines the lengths of both lists to align the starting points for a final traversal, ensuring that any comparison from then on checks nodes equidistant from the list ends. If the lists merge, the shared node is returned; otherwise, the function returns null, indicating no merge point.

6.13 Add Two Numbers

6.13.1 Problem

Write a program to add two numbers represented by linked lists
Example 1:
Input : List1 : 1->2->3 List2: 4->5
Output : 1->6->8

Example 2:
Input : List1 : 9->2->5 List2: 7->6
Output : 1->0->0->1

6.13.2 Algorithm

1. Initialize

   - Create a dummy head node dummyHead to simplify the handling of the result list's head.

   - Set two pointers p and q to the heads of the two input lists, l1 and l2, respectively.

   - Initialize a pointer curr to dummyHead, which will be used to build the result list.

   - Initialize an integer carry to 0, to keep track of the carry from the addition of two digits.

2. Iterate through Lists

   - While either p or q is not null (indicating there are more digits to process):

     - Retrieve the current digits x and y from p and q, respectively. If p or q is null, use 0 as the digit.

    – Calculate the sum of x, y, and carry.

    – Update carry to be the division of the sum by 10 (this is the carry for the next iteration).

    – Create a new node with the digit equal to the remainder of the sum divided by 10 and attach it to curr.next.

    – Advance curr to the next node.

    – Move p and q to their next nodes, if they are not null.

3. Handle Final Carry

- After exiting the loop, if there is a remaining carry (greater than 0), create a new node with the carry value and attach it to curr.next.

4. Return Result

- Return dummyHead.next, which points to the head of the result list.

6.13.3   Program

```
public ListNode addTwoNumbers(ListNode l1, ListNode l2)
    {
    ListNode dummyHead = new ListNode(0);
    ListNode p = l1, q = l2, curr = dummyHead;
    int carry = 0;
    while (p != null || q != null) {
        int x = (p != null) ? p.element : 0;
        int y = (q != null) ? q.element : 0;
        int sum = carry + x + y;
        carry = sum / 10;
        curr.next = new ListNode(sum % 10);
        curr = curr.next;
        if (p != null) p = p.next;
        if (q != null) q = q.next;
    }
    if (carry > 0) {
        curr.next = new ListNode(carry);
    }
    return dummyHead.next; // Return the next node of
    dummyHead, which is the head of the result list
    }
```

Listing 6.13: Add Two Numbers

6.13.4 Analysis

Time Complexity: $O(\max(m, n))$, where m and n are the lengths of the two input lists. The algorithm iterates through each list at most once, processing each digit exactly once, making the time complexity linear in the size of the input.

Space Complexity: $O(\max(m, n))$, since a new list is created to hold the result. In the worst case, the length of the result list is $\max(m, n) + 1$ (due to an extra carry), making the space complexity linear in the size of the input as well.

In Summary, this algorithm efficiently adds two numbers represented by linked lists, handling different lengths and carries between digits properly. The use of a dummy head node simplifies code logic and handling of edge cases.

6.14 Linked List Palindrome

6.14.1 Problem

Write a program to check the content of singly linked list is palindrome.

Example 1:
Input : 1 –> 2 –> 3 –> 2 –> 1
Output : true

Example 2:
Input : 1 –> 2 –> 3 –> 1
Output : false

Logic

We use fast and slow pointer technique to find the middle of the list, reversing the first half of the list as it progresses, and then comparing the first half with the second half. Here's a step-by-step Algorithm:

6.14.2 Algorithm

1. Initialize Pointers

- Two pointers, slow and fast, are initialized to the head of the list. The slow pointer moves one step at a time, while the fast pointer moves two steps at a time.

- A prev pointer is initialized to null to help in reversing the first half of the list.

2. Find Middle and Reverse First Half:

- While fast and fast.next are not null (indicating that the end of the list has not been reached), the algorithm progresses slow and fast pointers.

- As slow moves, the list from head to slow is reversed. prev acts as the new head of this reversed half.

- Once fast (moving twice as fast) reaches the end, slow will be at the midpoint of the list.

3. Adjust for Odd Number of Elements

- If the list has an odd number of elements, fast will not be null, and slow is moved one step forward to skip the middle element.

4. Compare Halves

- The second half of the list (starting from slow) is now compared with the reversed first half (pointed by prev).

- If at any point the values differ, the function returns false, indicating the list is not a palindrome.

- If all corresponding nodes in the two halves match, the loop completes, and the function returns true, indicating the list is a palindrome.

6.14.3   Program

```
public boolean isPalindrome(ListNode head) {
    ListNode slow, fast;
    slow=fast=head;
    ListNode prev = null;
    while(fast!=null && fast.next!=null) {
        ListNode next = slow.next;
```

```
8            fast = fast.next.next;
9            slow.next = prev;
10           prev = slow;
11           slow = next;
12       }
13       if(fast!=null){
14           slow = slow.next;
15       }
16
17       while(slow != null) {
18           if(slow.val != prev.val) {
19               return false;
20           }
21           slow = slow.next;
22           prev = prev.next;
23       }
24       return true;
25
26   }
```

Listing 6.14: Linked List Palindrome

6.14.4 Analysis

Time Complexity: O(n), where n is the number of elements in the list. The algorithm makes a single pass to find the midpoint and reverse the first half (O(n/2)), and another pass to compare the two halves (at most O(n/2)). Therefore, the overall time complexity is linear.

Space Complexity: O(1), as the algorithm uses a fixed number of pointers and modifies the list in-place without using any extra space proportional to the input size.

In Summary, this method is particularly effective because it achieves the goal with linear time complexity and constant space complexity, without needing to copy the list elements into a separate data structure for comparison.

6.15 Remove all occurrences

6.15.1 Problem

Write a program to remove all occurrences of given element in the singly linked list.

Example 1:
Input : 1 –> 2 –> 3 –> 2 –> 1, x=1
Output : 2 –> 3 –> 2

Example 2:
Input : 1 –> 1 –> 1 –> 2, x=1
Output : 2

6.15.2 Algorithm

1. Check for Empty List

   - If the list is empty (l == null), print "Empty List" and return null.

2. Remove Leading Occurrences

   - If the head of the list (l) contains the target value (x), move the head to the next node until the head does not contain x. This handles cases where the element to be removed is at the beginning of the list.

3. Initialize a Pointer

   - Set a current pointer to the (new) head of the list (l). This pointer is used to traverse the list starting from the head.

4. Traverse and Remove Occurrences

   - While current is not at the end of the list (current != null) and there's a next node (current.next != null)

     – If the next node contains the target value (current.next.element == x), remove the next node from the list by setting current.next to current.next.next. This effectively skips over the node containing x.

     – If the next node does not contain the target value, simply move the current pointer forward (current = current.next).

5. Return the Modified List

   - After traversing and removing all occurrences of x, return the head of the modified list (l).

6.15.3 Program

```
ListNode RemoveAllOccurances(ListNode l, int x) {
    if(l == null) {
        System.out.println("Empty List");
        return null;
    }
    while(l != null && l.element == x) {
        l = l.next;
    }
    ListNode current = l;
    while(current != null && current.next != null) {
        if(current.next.element == x) {
            current.next = current.next.next;
        } else {
            current = current.next;
        }
    }
    return l;
}
```

Listing 6.15: Remove all occurrences

6.15.4 Analysis

Time Complexity: The time complexity of this algorithm is O(n), where n is the number of nodes in the list. This is because, in the worst case, the algorithm traverses the entire list once to remove all occurrences of the target value.

Space Complexity: The space complexity is O(1) since no additional data structures are used for the traversal and removal process. The removal is done in-place by changing the pointers.

Efficiency: This algorithm is efficient in terms of both time and space complexity for removing all occurrences of a given value from a linked list. It directly manipulates the pointers within the nodes of the list to exclude nodes with the target value, thus avoiding the need for extra space or multiple traversals of the list.

6.16 Detect and Remove Loop in Linked List

6.16.1 Problem

Write an algorithm (or logic) to detect and remove loop in a singly linked list.

6.16.2 Algorithm

This approach is also dependent on Floyd's Cycle detection algorithm.
1. Detect Loop using Floyd's Cycle detection algo and get the pointer to a loop node.
2. Count the number of nodes in loop. Let the count be k.
3. Fix one pointer to the head and another to kth node from head.
4. Move both pointers at the same pace, they will meet at loop starting node.
5. Get pointer to the last node of loop and make next of it as NULL.

6.17 Copy Doubly Linked List

6.17.1 Problem

There is a doubly linked list with one pointer of each node pointing to the next node just like in a singly link list. The second pointer is pointing to any (arbitrary) node in the list.

Write a algorithm with O(n) time to create a copy of this list.

Arbitrary pointers are shown in red and next pointers in black

6.17.2 Algorithm

1. Create the copy of node 1 and insert it between node 1 and node 2 in original Linked List,
2. Create the copy of 2 and insert it between 2 and 3 and so on ..till the end.
3. Copy the arbitrary link as mentioned below
original->next->arbitrary = original->arbitrary->next;
4. Restore the original and copy linked lists as mentioned below in a single loop.

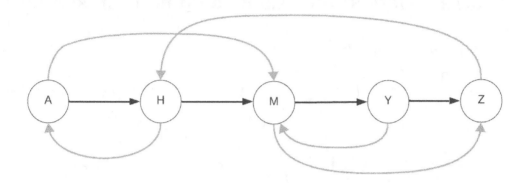

Figure 6.4: Copy a doubly linked list

original–>next = original–>next–>next;
copy–>next = copy–>next–>next;
5. Make sure that last element of original->next is NULL.

Chapter 7

Stacks and Queues

7.1 Introduction

7.1.1 Stack

A Stack is a linear data structure that serves as a collection of elements with the following main operations:

- Push, adds an element to the collection

- Pop, removes the most recently added element

- Peek, return the value of the last element added without modifying the stack

The order in which an element added to or removed from a stack is described as **L**ast **I**n, **F**irst **O**ut, most frequently referred as **LIFO**.

7.1.2 Queue

A queue is a linear data structure where elements are stored in the First In First Out(FIFO) principle. The following are main operations in a Queue:

- enqueue, adds an element to the rear of the queue

- dequeue, deletes an element from the front

- Peek (or front operation), returns the value of the next element to be dequeued without dequeuing it

The first element added to the queue will be the first one to be removed. This is equivalent to the requirement that once a new element is added, all elements that were added before have to be removed before the new element can be removed.

The data is inserted into the queue through one end (rear) and deleted from it using the other end (front) where as in stack both operations at one end.

7.2 Minimum Stack

7.2.1 Problem

Design a stack that supports push, pop, and retrieving the minimum element in constant time.

getMin() which should return minimum element from this special Stack.
Example 1:
Input : 10 −> top of stack
9
3
5
Output : getMin() : 3

Example 2:
Input : 15 −> top of stack
19
12
9
Output : getMin() : 9

7.2.2 Algorithm

This algorithm outlines the design of a special stack that, in addition to standard stack operations, supports a function getMin() that retrieves the minimum element in the stack in constant time. The implementation uses two stacks: stack for storing all the elements and minStack for keeping track of the minimum elements.

1. Push Operation (void push(int x)):

- Push the given element x onto the stack.

- If minStack is empty or x is less than or equal to the top element of minStack, push x onto minStack. This ensures minStack always holds the minimum element at its top.

2. Pop Operation (int pop()):

- If stack is empty, return -1 to indicate failure.

- Check if the top element of stack is equal to the top element of minStack. If so, pop the top element from minStack. This step maintains the integrity of minStack to ensure it always contains the current minimum of the stack.

- Pop and return the top element of stack.

3. Get Minimum Operation (int getMin()):

- If minStack is empty, return -1 to indicate that the stack is empty and there is no minimum.

- Otherwise, return the top element of minStack, which represents the minimum element in the stack.

7.2.3   Program

```java
public void push(int x) {
    stack.push(x);
    // Check if minStack is empty or x is less than or
    equal to the current minimum
    if (minStack.isEmpty() || x <= minStack.peek()) {
        minStack.push(x);
    }
}

public int pop() {
    if (stack.isEmpty()) return -1; // Return -1 or
    throw an exception if stack is empty
    int top = stack.pop();
    // If the popped element is the current minimum,
    pop it from minStack as well
    if (top == minStack.peek()) {
        minStack.pop();
    }
    return top;
}
```

```
20    public int getMin() {
21        if (minStack.isEmpty()) {
22            return -1; // Return -1 or throw an exception
      if minStack is empty
23        } else {
24            return minStack.peek(); // Retrieve the
      current minimum
25        }
26    }
```

Listing 7.1: Minimum Stack

7.2.4 Analysis

Time Complexity

- For push operation: $O(1)$ since adding an element to the top of a stack is a constant time operation.

- For pop operation: $O(1)$ since removing the top element of a stack and comparing top elements are both constant time operations.

- For getMin operation: $O(1)$ as it merely returns the top element of minStack.

Space Complexity

- $O(n)$, where n is the number of elements in the stack. In the worst-case scenario (e.g., when all the elements are pushed in non-increasing order), minStack could hold as many elements as the main stack.

Efficiency

- This Min Stack design is highly efficient in terms of time complexity, providing constant-time operations for adding elements, removing elements, and retrieving the minimum element.

- The trade-off comes in the form of increased space complexity due to the maintenance of an additional stack (minStack) to keep track of the minimum elements. However, this is a necessary trade-off to achieve the desired $O(1)$ time complexity for the getMin operation.

7.3 Valid Brackets

7.3.1 Problem

Given a string s containing just the characters '(', ')', '{', '}', '[' and ']', determine if the input string is valid with matching brackets.

An input string is valid if:

- Open brackets must be closed by the same type of brackets.

- Open brackets must be closed in the correct order.

Example 1:
Input : s = "()"
Output : true

Example 2:
Input : s = "()[]"
Output : true

Example 3:
Input : s = "(]"
Output : false

Example 4:
Input : s = "([)]"
Output : false

7.3.2 Algorithm

1. Initialization

   - Create a Stack<Character> to keep track of opening symbols.

   - Convert the input string s into a character array arr.

2. Iterate Through Characters

   - Loop through each character c in the array arr.

- If c is an opening symbol (’(’, ’{’, or ’[’), push it onto the stack.

3. Matching Closing Symbols

- If c is a closing symbol (’)’, ’}’, or ’]’):

    - Check if the stack is empty or the symbol at the top of the stack is not the corresponding opening symbol. If either condition is true, return false.

    - Otherwise, pop the top element from the stack as it matches the current closing symbol.

4. Final Check

- After iterating through all characters, check if the stack is empty. A non-empty stack indicates that there are unmatched opening symbols, so return false. If the stack is empty, all symbols were properly matched, so return true.

7.3.3   Program

```
public boolean isValid(String s) {
    Stack<Character> stack = new Stack<Character>();
    char[] arr = s.toCharArray();
    for(int i=0; i<arr.length; i++) {
        char c=arr[i];
        if(c=='(' || c=='{'|| c=='['){
            stack.push(c);
        }
        else if(c==')'){
            if(stack.isEmpty() || '('!=stack.pop()) {
                return false;
            }
        }
        else if(c=='}'){
            if(stack.isEmpty() || '{'!=stack.pop()) {
                return false;
            }
        }
        else if(c==']'){
            if(stack.isEmpty() || '['!=stack.pop()) {
                return false;
            }
        }
    }
    return stack.isEmpty();
```

```
27      }
```

Listing 7.2: Valid Brackets

7.3.4 Analysis

Time Complexity: O(n), where n is the length of the input string. The algorithm iterates through each character of the string exactly once.

Space Complexity: O(n) in the worst case, where n is the length of the input string. This would happen if all characters are opening symbols, requiring storage in the stack. However, in practice, the space usage will often be less than n because closing symbols do not get pushed onto the stack, and opening symbols are removed from the stack when matched.

Efficiency and Practicality

- The algorithm is efficient for validating strings containing parentheses, square brackets, and curly braces, providing a linear time solution.

- It uses a stack to ensure that symbols are correctly nested and matched, which is a straightforward and effective approach for this type of problem.

- The final check for an empty stack is crucial for handling cases where there are unmatched opening symbols, ensuring the correctness of the solution.

7.4 Palindrome

7.4.1 Problem

Check the content of singly linked list is palindrome or not.

Example 1:
Input : 1 -> 2-> 3->4->3->2->1
Output : True

Example 2:
Input : 1 -> 2-> 3->4->5->2->1
Output : False

7.4.2 Algorithm

This algorithm aims to determine whether the content of a singly linked list represents a palindrome. It utilizes a stack to compare the first half of the list with the second half in reverse order.

1. Initial Check

   - If the input linked list head is null, print "Empty List" and return false, indicating the list is not a palindrome.

2. Initialization

   - Create a Stack<ListNode> to store nodes of the linked list.

   - Use two pointers, slow and fast, both initially pointing to the head of the list.

3. First Half Processing

   - Traverse the list with slow moving one node at a time and fast moving two nodes at a time. This approach will place slow in the middle of the list by the time fast reaches the end.

   - Push nodes visited by slow onto the stack. This way, the stack will contain the first half of the list.

4. Handling Odd Number of Nodes

   - If fast is not null and fast.next is null (indicating an odd number of nodes), push the current slow node onto the stack to include the middle node in the palindrome check.

5. Second Half Processing

   - Continue moving slow through the second half of the list. For each node, pop a node from the stack (which contains nodes from the first half of the list) and compare the values.

   - If at any point the values do not match, return false, indicating the list is not a palindrome.

6. Palindrome Confirmation

   - If the loop completes without finding mismatches, return true, confirming the list is a palindrome.

7.4.3 Program

```
/**
 * Check the content of linked list is palindrome or
not
 *
 * @param l
 * @return
 */
public boolean Palindrome(ListNode head) {
    if(l==null){
        System.out.println("Empty List");
        return false;
    }
    else {
        Stack<ListNode> stack = new Stack<ListNode>();
        ListNode slow, fast;
        slow=fast=head;
        // add first half of list to stack with help
of slow and fast pointers
        while(slow!=null && fast!=null && fast.next!=
null) {
            // add to stack
            stack.add(slow);
            // increment slow pointer one node at a
time
            slow=slow.next;
            // increment fast pointer two nodes at a
time
            fast=fast.next.next;
        }
        // add to the stack if fast.next is null to
cover odd number of nodes case
        if(fast!=null && fast.next==null) {
            stack.add(slow);
        }
        // Compare second half of list with stack
values which contains first half of list
        while(!stack.isEmpty()) {
        // pop the node from stack
        ListNode temp = stack.pop();
        // check both the node values
        if(slow.element != temp.element) {
            return false;
        }
        // increment slow pointer by one node
        slow=slow.next;
        }
        // return as palindrome if all the nodes
matches
        return true;
```

```
43              }
44          }
```

Listing 7.3: Is Palindrome

7.4.4 Analysis

Time Complexity: $O(n)$, where n is the number of nodes in the linked list. The algorithm traverses the list twice at most: once to fill the stack (with slow and fast pointers) and once to compare the second half of the list with the stack content.

Space Complexity: $O(n/2){=}O(n)$ in the worst case, which simplifies to $O(n)$. This occurs because the stack stores half of the list's nodes. For lists with an odd number of nodes, it's essentially half the nodes rounded down, plus one.

Practical Considerations

- This algorithm efficiently checks if a list is a palindrome with linear time complexity and linear space complexity.

- The use of a stack is crucial for comparing the first half of the list in reverse order with the second half in its original order.

- Handling the middle node for lists with an odd number of nodes is essential for correctly identifying palindromes in such cases.

7.5 Median of Integers Stream

7.5.1 Problem

Find the median from stream of unsorted integers at any given point of time. We will be receiving a continuous stream of numbers in some random order and we don't know the stream length in advance.

Write a function that finds the median of the already received numbers efficiently at any time. We will be calling this program to find the median multiple times.

Just to recall, median is the middle element in an odd length sorted array, and the average of the middle elements in the even length case.

7.5.2   Logic for multiple solutions

1. Insertion Sort technique

Let's maintain sorted order of integers (make use of insertion sort technique). We can give the median as the middle element if the array length is odd, or the average of middle elements if the length is even. This can be done in O(1) time, but it takes O(N) time to keep the array sorted after inserting an element. We may need to shift the elements to the right, which will take O(N) time in worst case. Even though finding the position to insert the number takes O(logN) time, the overall insertion complexity is O(N) due to shifting.

2. Balanced Binary Search tree

let's use a balanced binary search tree to avoid worst case behaviour of standard binary search trees. In a height balanced binary search tree (i.e. AVL tree) the balance factor is the difference between the heights of left and right subtrees. A node with balance factor 0, +1, or -1 is considered to be balanced. However, in our tree the balance factor won't be height, it is the number of nodes in the left subtree minus the number of nodes in the right subtree. And only the nodes with balance factor of +1 or 0 are considered to be balanced. So, the number of nodes on the left subtree is either equal to or 1 more than the number of nodes on the right subtree, but not less.

If we ensure this balance factor on every node in the tree, then the root of the tree is the median, if the number of elements is odd. In the even case, the median is the average of the root and its inorder successor, which is the leftmost descendent of its right subtree. So, complexity of insertion maintaining balance condition is O(logN) and find median operation is O(1) assuming we calculate the inorder successor of the root at every insertion if the number of nodes is even. Insertion and balancing is very similar to AVL trees. Instead of updating the heights, we update the number of nodes information. Balanced binary search trees seem to be the most optimal solution as of now, insertion is O(logN) and find median is O(1).

3. Min-Heap and Max-heap

We can achieve the same complexity with a simpler and more elegant solution. We will use 2 heaps simultaneously, a max-heap and a min-heap with 2 requirements. The first requirement is that the max-heap contains the smallest half of the numbers and min-heap contains the largest half. So, the numbers in max-heap are always less than or equal to the numbers in min-heap. Let's call this the order requirement. The second requirement is that, the number of elements in max-heap is either equal to or 1 more than the number of elements in the min-heap. So, if we received 2N elements (even) up to now, max-heap and min-heap will both contain N elements. Otherwise, if we have received 2N+1 elements (odd), max-heap will contain N+1 and min-heap N. Let's call this the size requirement.

The max-heap for the values below the median, and a min-heap for the values above the median. When a new value arrives it is placed in the below heap (max-heap i.e. 1st half) if the value is less than or equal to the median, otherwise it is placed into the above heap (min-heap i.e. 2nd half). The heap sizes can be equal or the below heap (max-heap) has one extra. This constraint can easily be restored by shifting an element from one heap to the other. once we're asked for the median, if the total number of received elements is odd, the median is the root of the max-heap. If it's even, then the median is the average of the roots of the max-heap and min-heap. The median is available in constant time O(1) and insertion complexity is O(logN), which is the insertion complexity of a heap.

7.5.3 Algorithm

1. Initialization

   - Create two priority queues: minHeap to store the larger half of the numbers and maxHeap for the smaller half. maxHeap is a max-priority queue, which means it stores elements in descending order, while minHeap stores elements in ascending order.

2. Adding a New Number

   - **Determine the Target Heap**: If minHeap is empty or the new number num is greater than the smallest number in minHeap (i.e., minHeap.peek()), add num to minHeap. Otherwise, add it to maxHeap. This ensures that minHeap contains the larger half of the numbers, and maxHeap contains the smaller half.

- **Balance the Heaps**: After adding the new number, it's possible that the sizes of the two heaps differ by more than 1. To maintain a balanced state (where the size difference is no more than 1), transfer the top element from the larger heap to the smaller heap if necessary. This balancing step ensures that the median can be efficiently calculated.

3. Finding the Median

- **Single Median for Odd Total Count**: If the total count of numbers (sum of the sizes of minHeap and maxHeap) is odd, the median is the top element of the heap with more elements. This is straightforward because the larger heap effectively contains the middle element.

- **Average for Even Total Count**: If the total count is even, the median is the average of the two middle numbers, which are the top elements of both minHeap and maxHeap.

7.5.4   Program

```
1   public PriorityQueue<Integer> minHeap = new
        PriorityQueue<Integer>();
2   public PriorityQueue<Integer> maxHeap = new
        PriorityQueue<Integer>(Collections.reverseOrder());
3
4   public void addNum(int num) {
5       // Add to appropriate heap
6       if(minHeap.size()==0 || num > minHeap.peek()) {
7           minHeap.add(num);
8       } else {
9               maxHeap.add(num);
10      }
11
12      // Balance sizes of Min and Max Heaps
13      if(minHeap.size()>maxHeap.size()+1) {
14          maxHeap.add(minHeap.remove());
15      } else if(maxHeap.size()>minHeap.size()){
16          minHeap.add(maxHeap.remove());
17      }
18  }
19
20  public double findMedian() {
21      if(minHeap.size()>maxHeap.size()) {
22          return Double.valueOf(minHeap.peek());
23      }
24      else {
```

```
25          return (Double.valueOf(maxHeap.peek())+Double.
    valueOf(minHeap.peek())))/2;
26          }
27      }
```

Listing 7.4: Median of Integers Stream

7.5.5 Analysis

Time Complexity

Adding a Number (addNum): The time complexity is O(logn) due to the heap insertion operation, where O(logn) time for removal and insertion. Finding the Median (findMedian): The time complexity is O(1) because it involves only retrieving the top elements of the heaps and possibly calculating their average.

Space Complexity

O(n), where n is the number of elements in the data stream. This space is required to store the elements in the two heaps.

Practical Considerations

- This algorithm provides an efficient solution for finding the median in a running stream of data, which is particularly useful in scenarios where data is dynamically changing, and quick access to the median is required.

- The use of two heaps to separate the lower and upper halves of the data ensures that the median can always be calculated in constant time, making this approach highly efficient for real-time applications.

7.6 Exercises

1. Write a program to implement a first in first out (FIFO) queue using only two stacks. The implemented queue should support all the functions of a normal queue (push, peek, pop, and empty).

2. Write a program to return the length of the longest valid parentheses

from a given a string containing just the characters " and ",

3. Write a program to implement a stack using only two queues. The implemented stack should support all the functions of a normal stack (push, top, pop, and empty).

4. Given an array of size n. The task is to count the number of unique differences between the two maximum elements of every sub-array of size at least 2 of the given array.

5. Write a program to implement a stack-like data structure to push elements to the stack and pop the most frequent element from the stack.

.

Chapter 8

Binary Trees

8.1   Introduction

A binary tree is a non-linear data structure with a maximum of two children for each parent node. Each node in a binary tree has a left and right reference along with the data element. The node at the top of the tree is called a root node (A in Figure 8.1). The nodes that hold other sub-nodes are the parent nodes (B, C, E, F and root node A as well in Figure 8.1). The nodes that have no children are called leaf nodes (D, G, H and I nodes are leaf nodes in Figure 8.1).

8.2   Definition of Binary Tree Node

Binary Tree Node has an element to store value, references to left and right sub-trees.

```
1
2  public class TreeNode {
3
4    int element;
5    TreeNode left;
6    TreeNode right;
7
8    TreeNode(int n){
9      this(n, null, null);
10   }
11
12   TreeNode(int n, TreeNode l, TreeNode r) {
13     element = n;
14     left = l;
```

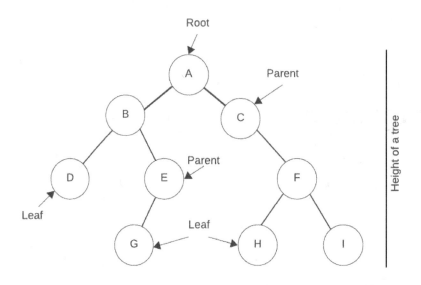

Figure 8.1: Binary Tree

```
15      right = r;
16    }
17 }
```

Listing 8.1: Binary Node

8.3 Print Binary Tree

This is a classic example of an in-order traversal of a binary tree. This type of traversal is one of the depth-first search (DFS) strategies for navigating through all the nodes in a binary tree. Here's how it works and its algorithmic analysis:

8.3.1 Algorithm

1. **Recursively Traverse the Left Subtree**: If the current node (referred to as T in your code) is not null, the algorithm first makes a recursive call to printTree(T.left), effectively processing all nodes in the left subtree before dealing with the current node. This step ensures that all nodes to the left of the current node are processed first, adhering to the in-order sequence (left, root, right).

2. **Process the Current Node**: Once the left subtree (if any) of the current node has been fully traversed, the method prints the value of

the current node (T.element). This represents the "root" part of the left-root-right in-order traversal pattern.

3. **Recursively Traverse the Right Subtree**: Finally, the method makes a recursive call to printTree(T.right), processing all nodes in the right subtree. This step is performed after the current node has been processed, ensuring that all nodes to the right of the current node are visited in the correct sequence.

8.3.2 Program

```
public void printTree(TreeNode T) {
  if(T!=null) {
    printTree(T.left);
    System.out.print(T.element + " ");
    printTree(T.right);
  }
}
```

Listing 8.2: Print Binary Tree

8.3.3 Analysis

Time Complexity: $O(n)$, where n is the number of nodes in the binary tree. This is because each node in the tree is visited exactly once during the in-order traversal.

Space Complexity: $O(h)$, where h is the height of the binary tree. This space complexity accounts for the call stack used during the recursive calls. In the worst-case scenario (a skewed tree), the space complexity could degrade to $O(n)$, but for balanced trees, it will be $O(\log n)$.

8.3.4 Practical Considerations

- In-order traversal is particularly useful when you need to process the nodes of a binary search tree (BST) in ascending order, as it leverages the inherent properties of BSTs (left < root < right).

- The method elegantly handles the traversal through recursive calls, showcasing the simplicity and power of recursion in tree algorithms.

- The printed output will be the elements of the tree sorted in ascending order if the tree is a binary search tree. For general binary trees, this method still applies but doesn't necessarily result in sorted output.

8.4   Count number of nodes in a Binary Tree

8.4.1   Algorithm

1. **Base Case - Empty Tree**: If the current node, referred to as T in your code, is null, the method returns 0. This base case is crucial for terminating the recursion when a leaf node's child (which doesn't exist) is accessed.

2. **Recursive Case - Non-empty Tree**: If the current node is not null, the method counts the node itself by adding 1 to the sum of the counts of nodes in the left and right sub-trees. This is achieved through the recursive calls countNodes(T.left) and countNodes(T.right), which explore the left and right sub-trees, respectively.

3. **Combine and Return Count**: The total count for the current sub-tree rooted at T is the sum of the counts of the left and right sub-trees plus one (for the current node itself). This value is returned to the caller.

8.4.2   Program

```
/**
 * Count number of nodes in a Binary Tree
 *
 * @param T
 * @return
 */
public int countNodes(TreeNode T) {
  if(T == null)
    return 0;
  else
    return countNodes(T.left)+countNodes(T.right)+1;
}
```

Listing 8.3: Count Nodes

8.4.3   Analysis

Time Complexity: O(n), where n is the number of nodes in the binary tree. This time complexity arises because the algorithm must visit each node exactly once to count it, effectively traversing the entire tree.

Space Complexity: O(h), where h is the height of the binary tree. The space complexity is dictated by the depth of the recursion, which in turn depends on the height of the tree. For a balanced tree, the height h = log(n), making the space complexity O(log(n)). For a skewed tree (worst-case scenario), the height can be as much as n (if every node has only one child), making the space complexity O(n).

Practical Considerations

- This program provides a clear example of how recursion can be used to simplify operations on binary trees, breaking down a complex problem into smaller, manageable sub problems.

- It's a generic method applicable to any binary tree, regardless of whether it's a binary search tree (BST), a balanced tree, or a skewed tree.

- The program efficiently combines the results from left and right subtrees, showcasing the divide-and-conquer strategy commonly used in tree algorithms.

8.5   Count number of leaf nodes

8.5.1   Algorithm

1. Base Case - Null Node

- If the current node T is null, it means the tree is empty or we've reached beyond the leaf nodes in a subtree. In this case, the method returns 0 since there are no leaf nodes to count.

2. Leaf Node Detection

- If the current node T is a leaf node (both T.left and T.right are null), the method returns 1. This signifies that one leaf node has been found.

3. Recursive Case - Internal Node

- If the current node is not a leaf node, the method recursively counts the number of leaf nodes in both the left and right subtrees of T and returns their sum. This is done by calling CountLeafNodes(T.left) and CountLeafNodes(T.right) and adding their results.

8.5.2   Program

```java
/**
 * Count number of leaf nodes
 *
 * @param T
 * @return
 */
public int CountLeafNodes(TreeNode T) {
  if(T == null) {
    return 0;
  }
  else if(T.left == null && T.right == null) {
    return 1;
  }
  else {
    return CountLeafNodes(T.left)+CountLeafNodes(T.right);
  }
}
```

Listing 8.4: Count Leaf Nodes

8.5.3   Analysis

Time Complexity

The time complexity of the method is $O(n)$, where n is the number of nodes in the binary tree. This is because the algorithm makes a single pass through all nodes in the tree, visiting each node exactly once to determine if it is a leaf.

Space Complexity

The space complexity is $O(h)$, where h is the height of the binary tree. This space is used by the call stack during the recursive calls. In the worst case (for a skewed tree), the space complexity could be $O(n)$, but for a balanced tree, it would be $O(\log n)$.

Summary

This program is a simple and efficient way to count the number of leaf nodes in a binary tree using recursion. Its design leverages basic properties of binary trees and demonstrates an effective use of recursion for tree traversal tasks.

8.6 Depth of Binary Tree

8.6.1 Algorithm

1. Base Case - Null Node

   - If the current node T is null, it means either the tree is empty or we've reached beyond the leaf nodes in a subtree. In this case, the method returns -1. This return value is chosen instead of 0 to correctly account for the depth as the number of edges (a single node has a depth of 0, so an empty tree has a depth of -1).

2. Recursive Case - Internal Node

   - If the current node is not null, the method recursively calculates the depth of both the left and right subtrees of T. It then returns the maximum of these two values plus one to account for the depth of the current node. The Max helper function is used to find the maximum between the left and right subtree depths.

8.6.2 Program

```
1
2   public int Max(int l, int r)
3   {
4      return l>r?l:r;
5   }
6
7   /**
8    * Depth of Binary Tree
9    *
10   * @param T
11   * @return
12   */
13  public int Depth(TreeNode T) {
14     if(T == null) {
15        return -1;
```

```
16      }
17      else {
18        return Max(Depth(T.left), Depth(T.right))+1;
19      }
20    }
```

Listing 8.5: Depth of Binary Tree

8.6.3 Analysis

Time Complexity

The time complexity of the Depth method is $O(n)$, where n is the number of nodes in the binary tree. This is because the algorithm makes a single pass through all nodes in the tree, visiting each node exactly once to calculate its depth.

Space Complexity

The space complexity is $O(h)$, where h is the height of the binary tree. This space is used by the call stack during the recursive calls. In the worst case (for a skewed tree), the space complexity could be $O(n)$, but for a balanced tree, it would be $O(\log n)$.

Summary

The Depth method efficiently computes the depth of a binary tree using recursion. By comparing the depths of the left and right subtrees and adding one for the current node, the method accurately calculates the overall depth of the tree. This method showcases the utility of recursion in solving tree-based problems by breaking them down into simpler subproblems.

8.7 Height of Binary Tree

8.7.1 Algorithm

1. Base Case - Null Node

   - If the current node T is null, the method returns -1. This accounts for the case where the tree is empty or when recursion reaches beyond the leaf nodes in a subtree. Returning -1 ensures that a tree with only a root node has a height of 0.

2. Recursive Case - Internal Node

- If the current node is not null, the method recursively calculates the height of both the left and right subtrees of T. It uses the Max function to determine the maximum height between these two subtrees and then adds one to account for the current node's edge.

8.7.2 Program

```java
/**
 * Height of Binary Tree
 *
 * @param T
 * @return
 */
public int Height(TreeNode T) {
  if(T==null) {
    return -1;
  }
  else {
    return Max(Height(T.left), Height(T.right))+1;
  }
}
```

Listing 8.6: Height of Binary Tree

8.7.3 Analysis

Time Complexity

The time complexity of the Height method is $O(n)$, where n is the number of nodes in the binary tree. This efficiency results from the algorithm traversing each node exactly once to compute its height, thereby making a complete pass through the tree.

Space Complexity

The space complexity is $O(h)$, where h is the height of the binary tree. This space is utilized by the call stack due to the recursive nature of the method. In the worst-case scenario (a skewed tree), the space complexity could degrade to $O(n)$. However, for a balanced binary tree, it would be more efficient, approximately $O(\log n)$.

Summary

The Height method is an effective recursive algorithm for computing the height of a binary tree. By examining the heights of the left and right subtrees and adjusting for the current node, it accurately determines the tree's overall height. This recursive approach is a classic example of how tree-based problems can be simplified into smaller, more manageable sub-problems, demonstrating the power and elegance of recursion in algorithm design.

8.8 Tree Traversals of a Binary Tree

Tree traversal is a process of visiting each node of a tree exactly once. It can perform an operation on the nodes like checking the node data, updating the node etc.

There are 4 types of tree traversal algorithms.

- Pre-order traversal

- In-order traversal

- Post-order traversal

- Level order traversal

8.8.1 Pre-order Traversal

Algorithm

1. Visit the current node.
2. Recursively traverse the current node's left sub-tree.
3. Recursively traverse the current node's right sub-tree.

Pre-order Traversal of Binary Tree in Figure 8.2 is A B D E G C F H I

```
1
2   /**
3    * PreOrder Traversal
4    *
5    * @param T
6    */
```

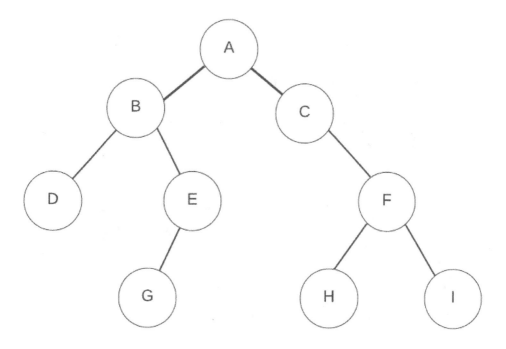

Figure 8.2: Tree Traversals

```
7    public void PreOrder(TreeNode T) {
8      if(T!=null) {
9        System.out.print(T.element + " ");
10       PreOrder(T.left);
11       PreOrder(T.right);
12     }
13   }
```

Listing 8.7: Pre-order Traversal

8.8.2   In-order Traversal

Algorithm

1. Recursively traverse the current node's left sub-tree.
2. Visit the current node.
3. Recursively traverse the current node's right sub-tree.

In-order Traversal of Binary Tree in Figure 8.2 is D B G E A C H F I

1

147

```
2    /**
3     * InOrder traversal
4     *
5     * @param T
6     */
7    public void InOrder(TreeNode T) {
8      if(T!=null) {
9        InOrder(T.left);
10       System.out.print(T.element + " ");
11       InOrder(T.right);
12     }
13   }
```

Listing 8.8: In-order Traversal

8.8.3 Post-order Traversal

Algorithm

1. Recursively traverse the current node's left sub-tree.
2. Recursively traverse the current node's right sub-tree.
3. Visit the current node.

Post-order Traversal of Binary Tree in Figure 8.2 is D G E B H I F C A

```
1
2    /**
3     * PreOrder Traversal
4     *
5     * @param T
6     */
7    public void PreOrder(TreeNode T) {
8      if(T!=null) {
9        System.out.print(T.element + " ");
10       PreOrder(T.left);
11       PreOrder(T.right);
12
13     }
14   }
```

Listing 8.9: Post-order Traversal

8.9 Level Order Traversal

8.9.1 Algorithm

1. Check for Empty Tree

   - Initially, check if the tree is empty (T == null). If it is, print "Empty Tree" and exit the method.

2. Initialization

   - Create a queue that will hold the nodes of the tree as they are being processed. The queue initially contains just the root node (T).

3. Traversal

   - While the queue is not empty, repeat the following steps:

     - Retrieve (but do not remove) the front node of the queue.
     - Print the element of the current node.
     - If the current node has a left child, add it to the queue.
     - If the current node has a right child, add it to the queue.
     - Remove the current node from the queue.

Level-Order Traversal of Tree in Figure 8.2 is A B C D E F G H I

8.9.2 Program

```
1
2    /**
3     * Level Order Traversal
4     *
5     * @param T
6     */
7    public void levelOrder(TreeNode T) {
8       if(T==null){
9          System.out.println("Empty Tree");
10         return;
11      }
12      else {
13         Queue<TreeNode> queue = new ArrayBlockingQueue<
      TreeNode>(50);
14         queue.add(T);
15         while(!queue.isEmpty()){
```

```
16      TreeNode node = queue.peek();
17      System.out.print(node.element + " ");
18      if(node.left!=null) {
19          queue.add(node.left);
20      }
21      if(node.right!=null) {
22          queue.add(node.right);
23      }
24      queue.remove();
25      }
26   }
27  }
```

8.9.3 Analysis

Time Complexity: O(n)
Every node in the tree is added to and removed from the queue exactly once. Therefore, the total time complexity is linear in the number of nodes in the tree, denoted by n.

Space Complexity: O(w)
The space complexity is determined by the maximum number of nodes that can be stored in the queue at any time, which corresponds to the widest level of the tree, denoted by w. In the worst case, a binary tree can be perfectly balanced, leading to a maximum width of O(n/2) for the last level, making the space complexity O(n) in such scenarios. However, for most practical purposes, especially in trees that are not perfectly balanced, the space complexity will be less than O(n).

Summary

The levelOrder method efficiently performs a level order traversal of a binary tree using a queue to keep track of the nodes at each level. This method ensures that all nodes are visited in their level order sequence, providing a comprehensive way to traverse and inspect the structure of a binary tree.

8.10 Zig Zag Level Order

8.10.1 Problem

Given a binary tree, print out the tree in Zig Zag level order (i.e, from left to right, then right to left for the next level and so on). Give a newline after the end of each level.

Zig-Zag level order traversal of Binary Tree in Figure 8.2 is below
A
C B
D E F
I H G

another example below:

```
      3
     / \
    9  20
      /  \
     15   7
```

the zig zag level order traversal of above tree is :
3
20 9
15 7

8.10.2 Logic

This problem can be solved easily using two stacks (one called currentLevel and the other one called nextLevel). You would also need a variable to keep track of the current level's order (whether it is left.right or right.left).

You can pop from stack currentLevel and print the node's value. Whenever the current level's order is from left.right, you push the node's left child, then its right child to stack nextLevel. Remember a Stack is a Last In First OUT (LIFO) structure, so the next time when nodes are popped off nextLevel, it will be in the reverse order.

On the other hand, when the current level's order is from right.left, you would push the node's right child first, then its left child. Finally, don't forget to swap those two stacks at the end of each level (i.e, when currentLevel is empty).

8.10.3 Algorithm

1. Initialization

   - Create two stacks, curLevel for the current level nodes and nextLevel for the nodes in the next level. Push the root node into curLevel and set a boolean leftToRight to true, indicating the direction of traversal for the current level.

2. Traversal

   - While curLevel is not empty, repeat the following steps:
     - Pop a node p from curLevel.
     - If p is not null, print p's value.
     - Depending on the value of leftToRight, push the child nodes of p into nextLevel. If leftToRight is true, push the left child first, then the right child. If leftToRight is false, push the right child first, then the left child.
     - When curLevel becomes empty (indicating the end of the current level), swap curLevel and nextLevel and toggle leftToRight to change the traversal direction for the next level.

3. Loop Termination

   - The loop terminates when there are no more nodes to process, i.e., when curLevel is empty after processing all nodes in nextLevel.

8.10.4 Program

```
/**
 * Zig Zag level order traversal
 *
 * @param T
 */
public void ZigZagOrder(TreeNode T)
{
    if(T==null) {
        System.out.println(" Empty Tree");
        return;
    }
    else {
        Stack<TreeNode> curLevel = new Stack<TreeNode>();
```

```
15    Stack<TreeNode> nextLevel = new Stack<TreeNode>();
16    curLevel.push(T);
17    boolean leftToRight=true;
18    while(!curLevel.isEmpty()) {
19      TreeNode p = curLevel.pop();
20      if(p!=null) {
21        System.out.print(p.element + " ");
22        if(leftToRight) {
23          nextLevel.push(p.left);
24          nextLevel.push(p.right);
25        }
26        else {
27          nextLevel.push(p.right);
28          nextLevel.push(p.left);
29        }
30      }
31      if(curLevel.isEmpty()) {
32        // change the order
33        leftToRight=!leftToRight;
34        // Swap curLevel and nextLevel
35        Stack<TreeNode> temp = curLevel;
36          curLevel = nextLevel;
37          nextLevel = temp;
38      }
39    }
40  }
41 }
```

Listing 8.10: Zig zag level order traversal

8.10.5 Analysis

Time Complexity: O(n)
Each node in the tree is visited exactly once, where n is the number of nodes. Therefore, the time complexity is O(n).

Space Complexity: O(n)
In the worst case, the space complexity can be O(n) when the tree is extremely unbalanced, and nearly half of the nodes are in the same level. However, for a balanced tree, the maximum size of the stacks combined will be proportional to the width of the tree at its widest point, which could still approach O(n) in the case of a complete binary tree.

Summary

The ZigZagOrder method is an effective way to traverse a binary tree in a zigzag fashion using two stacks to keep track of the current and next

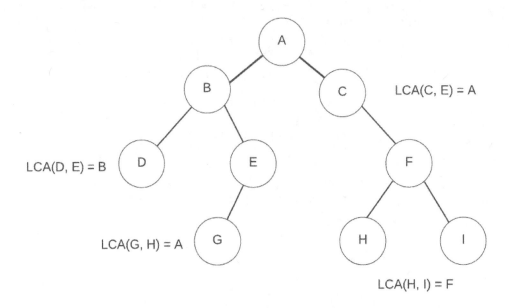

Figure 8.3: Lowest Common Ancestor in a Binary Tree

levels of the tree, efficiently managing the order of traversal by alternating between left to right and right to left at each level.

8.11 Lowest Common Ancestor

8.11.1 Problem

Write a program to find the lowest common ancestor (LCA) of two given nodes in a binary tree.

The lowest common ancestor is the lowest node in the tree that has both nodes n1 and n2 as descendants. Please refer figure 8.3 for examples.

8.11.2 Algorithm

1. Base case

   - If root is NULL, return NULL. If root is either p or q, return root. This indicates that we've found one of the nodes we're looking for.

2. Recursive calls

- Recursively search for p and q in the left subtree of root (L).

- Recursively search for p and q in the right subtree of root (R).

3. After both sub-trees evaluation

- After the recursive calls:

    - If both L and R are not NULL, it means p and q are found in different subtrees of root. Hence, root is their LCA.

    - If only one among L or R is not NULL, it means both p and q are located in the same subtree, and the non-NULL return value (L or R) is their LCA.

    - If both L and R are NULL, it means neither p nor q has been found in the current subtree rooted at root, and NULL is returned.

8.11.3 Program

```
TreeNode LCA(TreeNode root, TreeNode p, TreeNode q) {
  if (root == NULL) {
    return NULL;
  }
  if (root == p || root == q) {
    return root;
  }
  TreeNode L = LCA(root.left, p, q);
  TreeNode R = LCA(root.right, p, q);
  if (L != NULL && R != NULL) {
    return root;   // if p and q are on both sides
  }
  return (L != NULL) ? L : R;
}
```

Listing 8.11: Lowest Common Ancestor in a Binary Tree

8.11.4 Analysis

Time Complexity: O(n)

The function makes a single pass through the tree, where n is the number of nodes in the tree. Each node is visited exactly once, hence the time complexity is O(n).

Space Complexity: $O(h)$

The space complexity is proportional to the height of the tree h, due to the recursive call stack. In the worst case, for a skewed tree, the space complexity could be $O(n)$ (where n is the number of nodes, and the tree is essentially a linked list). For a balanced tree, it would be $O(\log n)$.

Summary

This LCA program efficiently finds the lowest common ancestor of two nodes in a binary tree using a single traversal, leveraging the properties of binary trees and recursion. Its performance is optimal in terms of both time and space, given the constraints of the problem.

8.12 Balanced Binary Search Tree

8.12.1 Problem

Write a program that creates a Balanced Binary Search Tree from a given sorted array using array elements.

```
Examples:
Input:  Array {1, 2, 3}
Output: A Balanced BST
     2
   /  \
  1    3

Input: Array {1, 2, 3, 4}
Output: A Balanced BST
     3
   /  \
  2    4
 /
1
```

8.12.2 Algorithm

1. **Base Condition**: If the left index is greater than the right index, it means the subarray is empty, and thus, should return NULL to signify

that no node will be created for this call.

2. **Choosing the Middle Element**: The middle element of the current subarray (defined by the left and right indices) is chosen as the root node for the current portion of the BST. This is done to ensure that the tree remains balanced. The middle is calculated as mid = left + (right - left) / 2 to avoid potential overflow that can occur with (left + right) / 2.

3. **Recursive Construction of Left Subtree**: The method is called recursively with the left half of the current subarray (left to mid - 1) to construct the left subtree, and the returned node is assigned as the left child of the current root.

4. **Recursive Construction of Right Subtree**: Similarly, the method is called recursively with the right half of the current subarray (mid + 1 to right) to construct the right subtree, and the returned node is assigned as the right child of the current root.

5. **Returning the Root**: Finally, the root node of the constructed subtree (or the entire tree if this is the initial call) is returned.

8.12.3   Program

```
 1
 2 public TreeNode sortedArrayToBalancedBST(int[] a, int left
   , int right) {
 3    if (left > right) {
 4       return null; // Use 'null' for Java, instead of '
   NULL'.
 5    }
 6
 7    int mid = left + (right - left) / 2;
 8    TreeNode root = new TreeNode(a[mid]);
 9
10    root.left = sortedArrayToBalancedBST(a, left, mid - 1)
   ;
11    root.right = sortedArrayToBalancedBST(a, mid + 1,
   right);
12
13    return root;
14 }
```

Listing 8.12: Create a Balanced Binary Search Tree

8.12.4   Analysis

Time Complexity: $O(n)$, where n is the number of elements in the array. Each element of the array is visited exactly once to create a corresponding node in the BST, making the time complexity linear.

Space Complexity: O(log n) for a balanced BST due to the recursion call stack. In the worst-case scenario (which this algorithm prevents by construction), it could be O(n), but since we're constructing a balanced BST, the height of the tree, and thus the depth of the recursion, will be log(n), where n is the number of elements in the array.

This method ensures that the constructed binary search tree is balanced, thereby optimizing the operations that can be performed on it.

8.13   Vertical Sum of a Binary Tree

8.13.1   Problem

Write a program to print vertical sum of the nodes that are in the same vertical line for a given Binary Tree. Please refer figure 8.4 for examples.

8.13.2   Algorithm

1. **Base Case**: If the current node T is null, terminate the recursion.

2. **Update TreeMap**: Add the value of the current node to its corresponding vertical level in treeMap. If the vertical level already exists, update its value by adding the current node's value.

3. **Recursive Calls**

- Recurse for the left subtree by decreasing the vertical level by 1 (vLevel - 1).

- Recurse for the right subtree by increasing the vertical level by 1 (vLevel + 1).

8.13.3   Program

```java
import java.util.TreeMap;

public class BinaryTree {

    public static TreeMap<Integer, Integer> treeMap = new
        TreeMap<>();
```

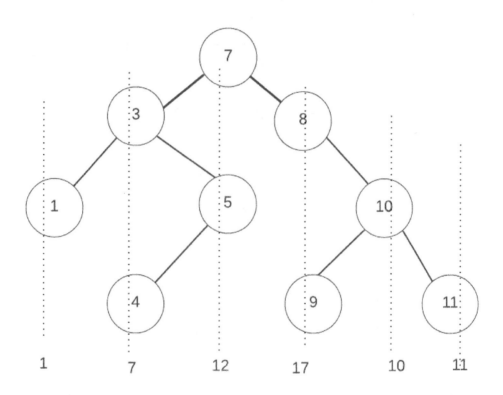

Figure 8.4: Vertical Sum of a Binary Tree

```
6
7    public void verticalSum(TreeNode T, int vLevel) {
8      if (T == null) {
9          return;
10     }
11
12     // Add the node's value to its corresponding vertical
       level in the TreeMap
13     treeMap.put(vLevel, treeMap.getOrDefault(vLevel, 0) +
       T.element);
14
15     // Recurse for left subtree with vertical level - 1
16     verticalSum(T.left, vLevel - 1);
17
18     // Recurse for right subtree with vertical level + 1
19     verticalSum(T.right, vLevel + 1);
20   }
21
22   public void printVerticalSum() {
23     for (Integer key : treeMap.keySet()) {
24         System.out.print(treeMap.get(key) + " ");
25     }
26   }
27 }
```

Listing 8.13: Vertical Sum of a Binary Tree

8.13.4 Analysis

8.13.5 Time Complexity

The verticalSum method visits each node exactly once. Therefore, the time complexity is $O(n)$, where n is the number of nodes in the binary tree. The printVerticalSum method iterates through the entries in treeMap. Let k be the number of vertical levels in the tree. Thus, its time complexity is $O(k)$. In the worst case, k can be n (consider a skewed tree), making the worst-case time complexity $O(n)$.

Space Complexity

The additional space used by the algorithm is for the recursion call stack and the treeMap. In the worst case, the height of the recursion call stack can be $O(n)$ for a skewed tree. The treeMap can have up to k entries, where k is the number of vertical levels. Therefore, the space complexity is $O(n + k)$. For a balanced tree, this would be more accurately described as $O(\log n + k)$ due to the height of the tree being log n.

Auxiliary Space

Apart from the input tree, the primary extra space is used by the treeMap for storing the sums, which is O(k).

Summary

This approach efficiently calculates and prints the vertical sum of a binary tree using depth-first search (DFS) for traversal and a TreeMap for keeping track of sums at different vertical levels.

8.14   Width of a Binary Tree

8.14.1   Problem

Write a program to get the maximum width of a binary tree. Width of a tree is maximum widths of all levels.

Let us consider the below example tree.

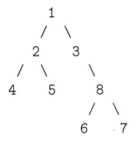

```
For the above tree,
    width of level 1 is 1,
    width of level 2 is 2,
    width of level 3 is 3
    width of level 4 is 2.
So the maximum width of the tree is 3.
```

8.14.2   Algorithm

1. height(TreeNode T):

  • Base Case: If the node T is null, the height is 0.

- For a non-null node, it recursively calculates the height of both the left and right subtrees, selects the maximum of these two values, and adds 1 (for the current node) to it.

2. getMaxWidth(TreeNode root):

- Initializes maxWidth to 0.

- It calculates the height of the tree to determine the number of levels.

- For each level from 1 to height, it calculates the width of that level using getWidth(TreeNode T, int level).

- Updates maxWidth if the current level's width is greater than the maxWidth.

3. getWidth(TreeNode T, int level):

- Base Case: If the node T is null, the width is 0.

- If level is 1, it means the function has reached the nodes of the desired level, so it returns 1.

- For levels greater than 1, it recursively calculates the width of the nodes at the level - 1 for both left and right subtrees and sums these widths.

8.14.3 Program

```java
public int height(TreeNode T) {
    if(T==null)
        return 0;
    return Math.max(height(T.left),height(T.right))+1;
}

public int getMaxWidth(TreeNode root) {
    int maxWidth=0;
    int height = height(root);
    for(int i=1; i<=height; i++) {
        int width=getWidth(root, i);
        if(width>maxWidth) {
            maxWidth=width;
        }
    }
    return maxWidth;
}
```

```
19
20    public int getWidth(TreeNode T, int level) {
21        if(T==null)
22            return 0;
23        if(level==1)
24            return 1;
25        else
26            return getWidth(T.left, level-1)+getWidth(T.
   right, level-1);
27
28    }
```

Listing 8.14: Width of a Binary Tree

8.14.4   Analysis

Time Complexity

The height function traverses the entire tree once, leading to O(n) time complexity, where n is the number of nodes in the binary tree.

The getMaxWidth function iterates through all levels of the tree, calling getWidth for each level. The getWidth function itself may traverse a significant portion of the tree for each call, especially for levels closer to the root. In the worst-case scenario, the total time taken can approach O(n*height) which simplifies to O(n log n) for a balanced tree but can be $O(n^2)$ for a skewed tree (where height is linear).

Space Complexity

The primary space consumption comes from the recursive call stack. The maximum depth of the recursion stack is bounded by the height of the tree for both the height and getWidth functions. Thus, the space complexity is O(height), which is O(log n) for a balanced tree but can be O(n) for a skewed tree.

No additional significant space is used, as the algorithm only maintains integer counters and does not use any data structures that grow with the size of the input.

Summary

This program efficiently calculates the maximum width of a binary tree, with its efficiency depending on the tree's structure. For balanced trees, it

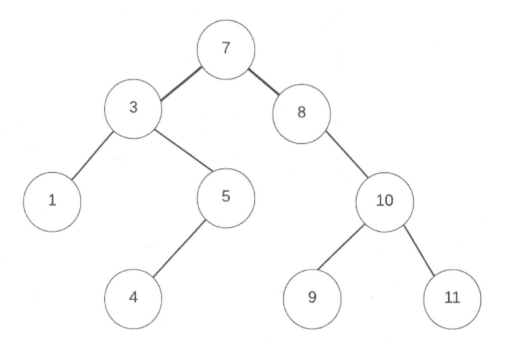

Figure 8.5: Binary Search Tree

operates more efficiently in terms of time complexity compared to skewed trees, where the performance can degrade.

8.15 Binary Search Tree

8.15.1 Introduction

A Binary Search Tree (BST) is a binary tree data structure with the following properties:

- All nodes of left sub-tree are less than the root node.

- All nodes of right sub-tree are more than the root node.

- Both left and right sub-tree of each node must also be a BST (i.e. it should satisfy above two properties)

Please refer figure 8.5 for an example BST.

8.16   Check Binary Search Tree

8.16.1   Problem

Write a program to check whether given binary tree is a binary search tree or not.

8.16.2   Algorithm

1. If the current node is null then return true
2. if the current node value is less than max value of left sub-tree then false
3. if the current node value is greater than min value of right sub-tree then false
4. Check left sub-tree and right sub-tree are also BST recursively

8.16.3   Program

Normal solution

```java
public boolean isBST(TreeNode T) {
    if(T == null){
        return true;
    }
    if(T.left != null && T.element < getMaxVal(T.left)) {
        return false;
    }
    if(T.right != null && T.element > getMinVal(T.right)) {
        return false;
    }
    return isBST(T.left) && isBST(T.right);
}

private int getMaxVal(TreeNode T){
    while(T.right != null) {
        T = T.right;
    }
    return T.element;
}

private int getMinVal(TreeNode T){
    while(T.left != null) {
```

```
23        T = T.left;
24      }
25      return T.element;
26   }
```

Listing 8.15: Check Binary Search Tree

Method 1: isBST(TreeNode T)

This method checks for every node if the tree is a BST by ensuring two conditions for each node:

All values on the left subtree of a node must be less than the node's value. All values on the right subtree of a node must be greater than the node's value. It uses two helper functions, getMaxVal(TreeNode T) and getMinVal(TreeNode T), to find the maximum value in the left subtree and the minimum value in the right subtree, respectively, and compares these values with the current node's value.

Correctness: This method correctly checks the BST property. However, it can be inefficient because it traverses down to the leaves for every node to find max and min values, causing a lot of redundant checks.

Time Complexity: Worse than $O(n)$. For every node, it traverses its subtrees to find max and min values, leading to a complexity closer to $O(n^2)$ in the worst case for a skewed tree.

Space Complexity: $O(h)$, where h is the height of the tree due to recursion. This could be $O(\log n)$ for a balanced tree and $O(n)$ for a skewed tree.

Efficient solution

```
1    public boolean isBST2(TreeNode T, int min, int max) {
2        if(T == null) {
3            return true;
4        }
5        if(min < T.element && T.element < max) {
6            return isBST2(T.left, min, T.element) &&
     isBST2(T.right, T.element, max);
7        }
8        else {
9            return false;
10       }
11   }
```

Listing 8.16: Check Binary Search Tree - Efficient

Method 2: isBST2(TreeNode T, int min, int max)

This method improves upon the first by keeping track of the minimum and maximum values that a node must be between to maintain the BST property. It's a more efficient way to ensure that every node's value is correctly placed within the range it's supposed to be, according to the BST rules.

Correctness: This method ensures that for every node, its value is within the valid range, which is updated as the recursion dives deeper. This effectively checks the BST property accurately.

Time Complexity: O(n), as it traverses each node exactly once.

Space Complexity: O(h), similar to the first method, where h is the height of the tree. The space complexity is due to recursion and remains O(log n) for a balanced tree and O(n) for a skewed tree.

Summary

The second method (isBST2) is generally preferred due to its better time complexity and more direct approach to checking the BST property. It avoids the redundancy of finding the max and min values for each subtree by efficiently using min and max bounds through recursion.

8.17   Lowest Common Ancestor of a BST

8.17.1   Problem

Write a program to find the lowest common ancestor (LCA) of two given nodes p and q in a Binary Search Tree (BST).

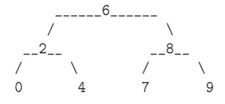

```
    / \
    3   5
```

For example, LCA of nodes 2 and 8 is 6.

Another example, LCA of nodes 2 and 4 is 2.

8.17.2   Algorithm

1. Start at the Root

    - Begin the search for the LCA from the root of the BST.

2. Search Left or Right

    - If both target nodes p and q have values less than the current node's value, move to the left child of the current node.

    - If both target nodes p and q have values greater than the current node's value, move to the right child of the current node.

3. Found LCA

    - If one target node's value is less than the current node's value and the other's is greater (or if one of the target nodes equals the current node), the current node is the LCA.

8.17.3   Program

```
1   public TreeNode lowestCommonAncestorBST(TreeNode root,
        TreeNode p, TreeNode q) {
2       if(root == null) {
3           return null;
4       }
5       if(p.element < root.element && q.element < root.
        element ) {
6           return lowestCommonAncestorBST(root.left, p, q
        );
7       }
8       else if(p.element > root.element && q.element >
        root.element) {
9           return lowestCommonAncestorBST(root.right, p,
        q);
10      } else {
11          return root;
```

```
12        }
13    }
```

Listing 8.17: Lowest Common Ancestor of a BST

8.17.4   Analysis

Time Complexity

The time complexity is O(h), where h is the height of the BST. This stems from the fact that the algorithm traverses the tree from root to leaf. In the best-case scenario (a balanced BST), this would be O(log n), with n being the number of nodes in the tree. In the worst-case scenario (a completely unbalanced BST), this would degrade to O(n).

Space Complexity

The space complexity is also O(h) due to the recursive call stack. In a balanced BST, this is O(log n), and in an unbalanced BST, it's O(n).

Key Points

BST Property Utilization: The algorithm leverages the BST property that left children are less than their parent and right children are greater. This property allows the algorithm to significantly reduce the search space, eliminating half of the tree with each step.

Efficiency: By only traversing from root to the specific leaf node, the algorithm ensures that each step is purposeful and minimizes unnecessary comparisons.

Simplicity: The algorithm is straightforward, relying on simple comparisons to direct the search for the LCA, making it both easy to understand and implement.

Summary

This program for finding the LCA in a BST is efficient due to its use of the BST properties, with its performance hinging on the height of the tree. This makes it particularly effective for balanced BSTs, where the height is minimized.

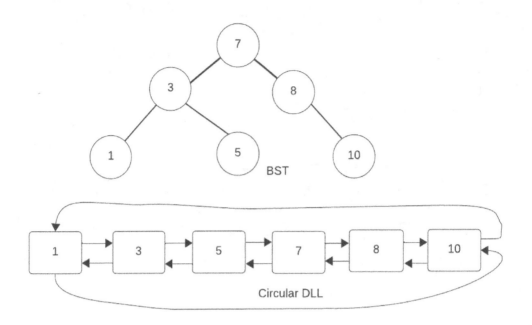

Figure 8.6: Convert BST to Circular Doubly Linked List

8.18 Convert BST to Doubly Linked List

8.18.1 Problem

Convert a BST to a sorted circular doubly linked list in-place.

8.18.2 Algorithm

1. Base Case

   - If the root is null, return null. This step handles empty trees.

2. Recursive Transformation

   - Recursively convert the left subtree of the root into a circular doubly linked list (denoted as aList).

   - Recursively convert the right subtree of the root into a circular doubly linked list (denoted as bList).

3. Root Conversion

- Convert the root node into a circular doubly linked list by making its left and right pointers point to itself.

4. List Appending

- Append aList (left list) with the root node, and then append the result with bList (right list). This forms a single circular doubly linked list that maintains the in-order sequence of the BST.

5. Append Functionality

- If either list to be appended is null, return the other list.

- Find the last nodes of both lists (aLast and bLast) by accessing their left pointers.

- Join aLast with the beginning of b, and bLast with the beginning of a, effectively merging the two lists into a circular doubly linked list.

6. Join Functionality

- Given two nodes, a and b, set a's right pointer to b and b's left pointer to a, effectively linking them in a circular manner.

8.18.3 Program

```
1
2 /**
3    * Given an binary search tree (bst), recursively change
     it into a circular doubly linked list
4    *
5    * @param root
6    * @return
7    */
8 public Node treeToList(Node root) {
9        // base case: empty tree -> empty list
10       if (root==null) {
11         return null;
12       }
13
14       // Recursively do the subtrees
15       Node aList = treeToList(root.left);
16       Node bList = treeToList(root.right);
17
18       // Make the single root node into a list
```

```
19          root.left = root;
20          root.right = root;
21
22          // At this point we have three lists, and it's
23          // just a matter of appending them together
24          // in the right order (aList, root, bList)
25          aList = append(aList, root);
26          aList = append(aList, bList);
27
28          return aList;
29      }
30
31  public Node append(Node a, Node b) {
32          // if either is null, return the other
33          if (a==null) {
34            return b;
35          }
36          if (b==null) {
37            return a;
38          }
39
40          // find the last node in each list using the left
    pointer
41          Node aLast = a.left;
42          Node bLast = b.left;
43
44          // join the two together to make it connected and
    circular
45          join(aLast, b);
46          join(bLast, a);
47
48          return(a);
49      }
50
51  /**
52   * helper function -- given two list nodes, join them
53      * together so the second immediately follow the first
54      * Sets the .right of the first and the .left of the
    second.
55   *
56   * @param a
57   * @param b
58   */
59  public void join(Node a, Node b) {
60          a.right = b;
61          b.left = a;
62      }
```

Listing 8.18: Convert BST to Doubly Linked List

8.18.4 Analysis

Time Complexity: $O(n)$, where n is the number of nodes in the BST. Each node is visited exactly once, making the algorithm linear in the number of nodes.

Space Complexity: $O(h)$, where h is the height of the BST. This space is used by the call stack during the recursive calls. In the worst case (a skewed tree), this becomes $O(n)$, and in the best case (a balanced tree), this is $O(\log n)$.

Key Points

The program maintains the in-order sequence of the nodes from the BST in the transformed circular doubly linked list, which is crucial for retaining the sorted order.

The transformation is done in-place with respect to the nodes themselves, but requires recursive stack space.

The resulting circular doubly linked list has its end connected back to the beginning, forming a circular structure.

8.19 Boundary nodes of a Binary Tree

8.19.1 Problem

Print all edge nodes of a complete binary tree anti-clockwise. That is all the left most nodes starting at root, then the leaves left to right and finally all the rightmost nodes.

8.19.2 Algorithm

1. Print the Root Node

   - Begin by printing the root node of the tree if it is not null. This step ensures that the top boundary (which, in this case, is just the root node) is covered.

2. Print Left Boundary

- Recursively traverse the left part of the tree to print the left boundary. Start from the root's left child to avoid reprinting the root.

- For each node encountered, print it if it's either a boundary node (non-leaf) or a leaf node. This is determined by the print flag and the presence of child nodes.

- The recursion goes deeper first into the left subtree and then into the right subtree when there's no left child, ensuring no boundary nodes are missed.

3. Print Right Boundary

- Similar to the left boundary but start from the root's right child.

- Traverse the tree in a manner that you first go deep into the right subtree, then the left subtree when there's no right child, ensuring you're on the boundary.

- Print the nodes in reverse order, ensuring the bottom-most right boundary node is printed first, climbing up to the root.

4. Combining Left and Right Boundaries

- The printOuterEdges function orchestrates the printing by first printing the root, then invoking the methods to print the left boundary and right boundary respectively.

- Leaf nodes are handled implicitly and printed either in the left or right boundary printing phase, ensuring no leaf node is printed twice.

8.19.3   Program

```java
public void printLeftEdges(BinaryNode p, boolean print) {
    if (p == null) return;
    if (print || (p.left == null && p.right == null))
        System.out.print(" " + p.element);
    printLeftEdges(p.left, print);
    printLeftEdges(p.right, (print && p.left == null));
}

public void printRightEdges(BinaryNode p, boolean print) {
    if (p == null) return;
    printRightEdges(p.left, (print && p.right == null));
```

```
13     printRightEdges(p.right, print);
14     if (print || (p.left == null && p.right == null))
15         System.out.print(" " + p.element);
16 }
17
18 public void printOuterEdges(BinaryNode root) {
19     if (root == null) return;
20         System.out.print(root.element);
21     printLeftEdges(root.left, true);
22     printRightEdges(root.right, true);
23 }
```

Listing 8.19: Boundary nodes of a Binary Tree

8.19.4 Analysis

Time Complexity: The algorithm has a time complexity of $O(n)$, where n is the number of nodes in the binary tree. Each node is visited exactly once during the process of printing the left and right boundaries.

Space Complexity: The space complexity is $O(h)$ due to the recursion stack, where h is the height of the binary tree. In the worst-case scenario of a skewed tree, this becomes $O(n)$, but in a balanced tree, it would be $O(\log n)$.

Summary

The program efficiently prints all outer edges of a binary tree by separately handling the left and right boundaries and ensuring that all edge nodes, including the leaf nodes, are covered without duplication. The recursive approach allows for a straightforward traversal while maintaining the order of printing from top to bottom for the left boundary and bottom to top for the right boundary, thus ensuring a complete outline of the tree's boundary is printed.

8.20 Next Right Pointers

8.20.1 Problem

Write a program to populate Next Right Pointers in Each Node in a Binary Tree.

For example,

Given the following binary tree,

```
      1
    /   \
   2     3
  / \     \
 4   5     7
```

After calling your function, the tree should look like:

```
      1 -> NULL
    /   \
   2 -> 3 -> NULL
  / \     \
 4-> 5 -> 7 -> NULL
```

8.20.2   Algorithm

1. Initialization

   - Start by checking if the root is null. If it is, return immediately as there are no nodes to connect. Initialize a queue that will hold nodes to be processed.

2. Root Processing

   - Add the root node to the queue and also add a null marker right after it. This null serves as a level delimiter indicating the end of a level in the tree.

3. Level Order Traversal with Connections

   - While the queue is not empty, repeatedly dequeue an element.

   - For a dequeued node that is not null, set its next field to the next element in the queue. This operation connects the node to its immediate right neighbor.

   - Add the node's left and right children to the queue if they exist.

   - When a null element is dequeued (indicating the end of a level), and the queue is not empty (indicating there are more levels to process), enqueue another null to mark the end of the next level.

4. Termination

   - The loop terminates when the queue becomes empty, which means all nodes have been processed and connected appropriately.

8.20.3   Program

```
1 public void connect(TreeLinkNode root) {
2     Queue<TreeLinkNode> queue = new LinkedList<
      TreeLinkNode>();
3
4         if(root==null)
5             return;
6         queue.add(root);
7         // add null to remember level
8         queue.add(null);
9         while(!queue.isEmpty()) {
10            TreeLinkNode temp = queue.poll();
11            if(temp!=null) {
12                temp.next = queue.peek();
13                if(temp.left!=null) {
14                    queue.add(temp.left);
15                }
16                if(temp.right!=null) {
17                    queue.add(temp.right);
18                }
19            }
20            // if queue is not empty, push NULL to mark
      nodes at this level are visited
21            else if(!queue.isEmpty()) {
22                queue.add(null);
23            }
24
25        }
26    }
```

Listing 8.20: Next Right Pointers in a Binary Tree

8.20.4   Analysis

Time Complexity: O(N), where N is the number of nodes in the binary tree. Each node is enqueued and dequeued exactly once, ensuring that every node is visited and connected to its right neighbor.

Space Complexity: O(W), where W is the maximum width of the binary tree. This is because the maximum number of elements that can be in the queue at any time is determined by the widest level of the tree. In the worst-case scenario (a perfectly balanced binary tree), this would be roughly half of the total number of nodes.

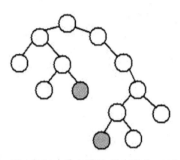
diameter, 9 nodes, through root

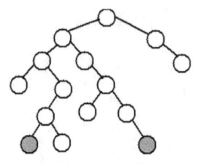
diameter, 9 nodes, NOT through root

Figure 8.7: Diameter of a Binary Tree

Summary

The program effectively utilizes a BFS approach with a queue to traverse the tree level by level and connect nodes horizontally within the same level. It smartly uses a null marker to identify the end of each level, allowing for the connection of nodes without additional space for tracking node levels. The overall time efficiency is linear with respect to the number of nodes, and the space efficiency is optimal with respect to the tree's width, making it a practical solution for the problem at hand.

8.21 Diameter of a Binary Tree

8.21.1 Problem

The diameter of a tree (sometimes called the width) is the number of nodes on the longest path between two leaves in the tree. The Figure 8.7 below shows two trees each with diameter nine, the leaves that form the ends of a longest path are shaded (note that there is more than one path in each tree of length nine, but no path longer than nine nodes).

8.21.2 Algorithm

1. Base Case

   - If the root is null, the height of the tree is 0, and thus the diameter at this point is also considered to be 0.

2. Calculate Heights

- For each node (starting from the root), calculate the height of its left and right subtrees. The height of a tree is the length of the longest path from the root to a leaf.

3. Calculate Diameters

- Recursively calculate the diameter of the left and right subtrees. This allows the algorithm to consider the longest path that might not pass through the root node.

4. Compute Maximum Diameter

- The diameter of the tree at the current node can be considered as either:

  − The longest path that goes through the current node, which is the sum of the heights of the left and right subtrees plus 1 (for the root node itself), or

  − The maximum diameter of the left or right subtree, which accounts for the longest path that does not pass through the current node.

- The final diameter is the maximum of these two values.

8.21.3 Program

```
public int getHeight(Node root) {
    if (root == null)
        return 0;
    return Math.max(getHeight(root.left), getHeight(root.
    right))+1;
}

public int Diameter(Node root) {
  if (root == null)
      return 0;

  // get the left and right subtree height
  int leftSubTree = getHeight(root.left);
  int rightSubTree = getHeight(root.right);

  // get the left diameter and right diameter recursively.
  int leftDiameter = Diameter(root.left);
  int rightDiameter = Diameter(root.right);

  // get the max leftsubtree, rightsubtree, longest path
  goes through root.
```

```
20    return Math.max(leftSubTree+rightSubTree+1, Math.max(
         leftDiameter, rightDiameter));
21 }
```

Listing 8.21: Diameter of a Binary Tree

8.21.4   Analysis

Time Complexity: $O(N^2)$ in the worst case, where N is the number of nodes in the binary tree. This is because for every node, the getHeight function is called which traverses the subtree of that node. Hence, for each node, we perform a traversal of all the nodes beneath it, leading to a quadratic time complexity.

Space Complexity: $O(H)$, where H is the height of the tree. This space is used by the recursion stack. In the worst case (for a skewed tree), the space complexity would be $O(N)$.

Optimization

To optimize this algorithm, one could compute the height and diameter of the subtree in a single recursion rather than computing heights separately. This approach reduces the time complexity to $O(N)$ because each node is visited only once.

Summary

While the algorithm correctly calculates the diameter of a binary tree, its efficiency can be significantly improved by combining the height calculation and the diameter calculation into a single recursion, thereby reducing the overall time complexity from $O(N^2)$ to $O(N)$, which is essential for handling large trees efficiently.

8.22   Mirror of a Binary Tree

8.22.1   Problem

Mirror of a Binary Tree T is another Binary Tree M(T) with left and right children of all non-leaf nodes interchanged.

8.22.2   Algorithm

1. Base Case Check

   - If the current node (T) is null, the function returns immediately. This base case is essential for recursion and ensures that the function eventually terminates when it reaches leaf nodes.

2. Recursive Calls

   - The function first calls itself recursively on the left child of the current node (T.left), then on the right child (T.right). These recursive calls ensure that all nodes in both subtrees are visited and their children are swapped.

3. Swapping Children

   - After the recursive calls return (meaning the subtrees have been mirrored), the function swaps the left and right children of the current node. This is done by using a temporary variable (temp) to hold one of the children during the swap.

8.22.3   Program

```
void mirror(TreeNode T) {
    If(T != null) {

        // do the subtrees recursively
        mirror(T.left);
        mirror(T.right);

        // swap the pointers in this node
        TreeNode temp = T.left;
        T.left = T.right;
        T.right = temp;
    }

}
```

Listing 8.22: Mirror of a Binary Tree

8.22.4 Analysis

Time Complexity

The time complexity of the mirror function is O(N), where N is the number of nodes in the tree. This is because the algorithm visits each node exactly once. The visit involves constant-time operations (specifically, the swap operation), so the overall time complexity is linear in the number of nodes.

Space Complexity

The space complexity is O(H), where H is the height of the tree. This space is used by the call stack during the recursion. In the worst case (a skewed tree), this could be O(N), but for a balanced tree, it would be O(log N).

Summary

This program effectively generates the mirror image of a binary tree by recursively swapping the left and right children of each node. Its implementation is straightforward and efficient, with linear time complexity and space complexity dependent on the tree's height. This transformation is done in place, modifying the original tree structure.

8.23   Height Balanced Binary Tree

8.23.1   Problem

Write a program to check if it is a height-balanced tree.

For this problem, a height-balanced binary tree is defined as: a binary tree in which the depth of the two subtrees of every node never differ by more than 1.

8.23.2   Algorithm

1. Base Case

   - If the current node (root) is null, the tree is trivially balanced, so it returns true.

2. Calculate Subtree Heights

- The height of the left and right subtrees are calculated using the height method. If the subtree is null, its height is considered -1.

3. Check Height Difference

- If the absolute difference between the left and right subtree heights is more than 1, the tree is not balanced, and the method returns false.

4. Recursive Checks

- The method then recursively checks if the left and right subtrees are balanced.

5. Return Value

- The method returns true if both subtrees are balanced; otherwise, it returns false.

8.23.3   Program

```
public boolean isBalanced(TreeNode root) {

    if(root == null) {
        return true;
    }
    int lHeight = -1, rHeight = -1;
    if(root.left != null) {
        lHeight = height(root.left);
    }

    if(root.right != null) {
        rHeight = height(root.right);
    }
    if(Math.abs(lHeight-rHeight)>1) {
        return false;
    }
    return isBalanced(root.left)&&isBalanced(root.right);
    }

    private int height(TreeNode T) {
        if(T == null) {
            return -1;
```

```
24          }
25          if(T.left==null && T.right==null) {
26              return 0;
27          }
28          return Math.max(height(T.left),height(T.right))+1;
29      }
```

Listing 8.23: Height Balanced Binary Tree

8.23.4 Analysis

Time Complexity

The time complexity of this method is $O(N^2)$ in the worst case, primarily due to the repeated calculation of heights for subtrees. For each node, the height method potentially traverses all its descendants, leading to quadratic behavior in terms of the number of nodes (N).

Space Complexity

The space complexity is $O(H)$, where H is the height of the tree. This space is used by the call stack due to recursion. In the worst case (a skewed tree), this could be $O(N)$, but for a balanced tree, it would be $O(\log N)$.

Optimization

The approach can be optimized to $O(N)$ by modifying the height method to check the balance condition during height calculation, thus avoiding the need for separate height calculations for each node. This optimization involves returning a special value (e.g., -1) to indicate that a subtree is unbalanced, allowing the balance check and height calculation to be combined into a single pass through the tree.

8.24 Construct BT from Inorder and Preorder

8.24.1 Problem

Construct a binary tree from a given inorder and preorder traversals.

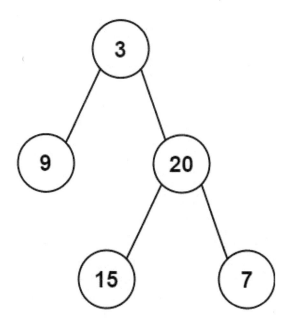

Figure 8.8: Construct Binary tree

Example 1:
Input : inorder = {9,3,15,20,7} preorder = {3,9,20,15,7}
Output : {3,9,20,null,null,15,7}

Example 2:
Input : inorder = {1} preorder = {1}
Output : {1}

8.24.2 Algorithm

1. Hashmap Preparation

- The algorithm starts by creating a hashmap (inorderMap) that stores the indices of elements in the inorder array. This step is crucial for efficiently finding the position of each element in the inorder sequence, which is needed to partition the tree into left and right subtrees.

2. Base Case

- The recursion base case is when the left index is greater than the right index, indicating that the subtree is empty. In this case, the method returns null.

3. Recursive Tree Construction

- The buildTree method initiates the recursive construction process by calling the inorderPreorderTree helper method, passing the entire range of the preorder array as the initial segment to consider.

4. Building Subtrees

- The recursive helper method inorderPreorderTree constructs the tree in a top-down manner, starting from the root. It uses the index variable to keep track of the current root node in the preorder array.

- It creates a new TreeNode for each recursive call using the current value pointed by index in the preorder array, then increments index.

- The position of this root in the inorder array is found using inorderMap. This position splits the inorder array into left and right subtrees.

- The method then recursively constructs the left and right subtrees by appropriately adjusting the left and right bounds for the inorder array segments.

8.24.3　Program

```
1    private Map<Integer, Integer> inorderMap = new HashMap<
         Integer, Integer>();
2    private int index=0;
3
4    public TreeNode buildTree(int[] preorder, int[] inorder)
         {
5        // build hashmap with inorder indexes
6        for(int i=0; i<inorder.length; i++) {
7            inorderMap.put(inorder[i],i);
8        }
9        return inorderPreorderTree(inorder, preorder, 0,
         preorder.length-1);
10   }
11
12   private TreeNode inorderPreorderTree(int[] inorder, int
         [] preorder, int left, int right {
13       if(left > right) {
14           return null;
15       }
16       int rootVal = preorder[index++];
17       TreeNode root = new TreeNode(rootVal);
18
19       root.left = inorderPreorderTree(inorder, preorder,
         left, inorderMap.get(rootVal)-1);
```

```
20          root.right = inorderPreorderTree(inorder, preorder
        , inorderMap.get(rootVal)+1, right);

21

22          return root;

23    }
```

Listing 8.24: Construct Binary Tree from Inorder and Preorder Traversals

8.24.4   Analysis

Time Complexity

O(N): The algorithm has a linear time complexity, where N is the number of nodes in the tree. This efficiency is achieved by using the hashmap for instant lookup of root positions in the inorder array, avoiding the need for a linear search which would otherwise result in $O(N^2)$ complexity for unbalanced trees.

Space Complexity

O(N): The space complexity is also linear due to the storage requirements of the hashmap and the recursion call stack. In the worst case, the space taken by the call stack is proportional to the height of the tree, which can be O(N) in the case of a skewed tree. The hashmap also stores N key-value pairs.

Correctness

The algorithm correctly constructs the binary tree by ensuring that each node is placed according to its preorder and inorder positions, effectively reconstructing the original binary tree structure.

Optimization

The use of a hashmap for index lookup is a significant optimization for this problem, reducing the time complexity from quadratic to linear by eliminating the need for repeated scanning of the inorder array.

8.25 Construct BT from Inorder and Postorder

8.25.1 Problem

Construct a binary tree from a given inorder and postorder traversals.
Example 1:
Input : inorder = {9,3,15,20,7} postorder = {9,15,7,20,3}
Output : {3,9,20,null,null,15,7}

Example 2:
Input : inorder = {1, 2, 3} postorder = {2, 3, 1}
Output : {1, 2, 3}

8.25.2 Algorithm

1. Initialization

   - Create a hashmap (inorderMap) to store the index of each value in the inorder traversal for quick lookup. This reduces the search time for finding the root node in the inorder array from $O(n)$ to $O(1)$.

2. Build Tree

   - Starting with the last element in the postorder array (which is the root of the tree), recursively construct the tree by finding the root in the inorder array using the hashmap. This divides the inorder array into left and right subtrees.

3. Recursive Construction

   - For each node, find the index in the inorder array using inorderMap.

   - Recursively construct the right subtree using the index found plus one to the end of the current segment.

   - Recursively construct the left subtree from the start of the current segment to the found index minus one.

   - Decrement the index for the postorder array in each recursive call to move to the next root node.

4. Termination

   - The recursion ends when the left index is greater than the right index, indicating that there are no elements to construct a subtree.

8.25.3 Program

```
1    private Map<Integer, Integer> inorderMap = new HashMap
     <Integer, Integer>();
2    private int index;
3
4    public TreeNode buildTree(int[] inorder, int[]
     postorder) {
5        index = postorder.length-1;
6
7        // build hashmap with inorder indexes
8        for(int i=0; i<inorder.length; i++) {
9            inorderMap.put(inorder[i],i);
10       }
11
12       return inorderPostorderTree(inorder, postorder, 0,
     postorder.length-1);
13   }
14
15   private TreeNode inorderPostorderTree(int[] inorder,
     int[] postorder, int left, int right ) {
16       if(left > right) {
17           return null;
18       }
19
20       int rootVal = postorder[index--];
21       TreeNode root = new TreeNode(rootVal);
22
23       root.right = inorderPostorderTree(inorder,
     postorder, inorderMap.get(rootVal)+1, right);
24       root.left = inorderPostorderTree(inorder,
     postorder, left, inorderMap.get(rootVal)-1);
25
26       return root;
27   }
```

Listing 8.25: Construct Binary Tree from Inorder and Postorder

8.25.4 Analysis

Time Complexity: O(n), where n is the number of nodes in the tree. Even though there are recursive calls, each node is processed exactly once due to the linear structure of the inorder and postorder arrays. The hashmap allows for constant time lookup of the root's index in the inorder array.

Space Complexity: O(n) for the hashmap storage plus the recursion stack. The hashmap stores each node's value and index from the inorder traversal. The maximum depth of the recursion stack is $O(h)$, where h is the height of the tree, contributing to the space complexity. In the worst case, the tree might be skewed, making the height h equal to n, thus making the total space complexity $O(n)$ due to the hashmap being the dominant factor.

Summary

This program efficiently reconstructs a binary tree from its inorder and postorder traversals by using a hashmap for quick lookup of root positions in the inorder array, facilitating a divide-and-conquer approach to build the tree recursively.

References

[1] Weiss, Mark A. (2012) *Data Structures & Algorithm Analysis in C++*, Pearson Education.

[2] https://vchenna.wordpress.com/

[3] https://www.wikipedia.org/

[4] https://hadoopnalgos.blogspot.com/

[5] https://www.geeksforgeeks.org/

[6] Cormen, Thomas H. and Leiserson, Charles E. and Rivest, Ronald L. and Stein, Clifford (2009) *Introduction to Algorithms, Third Edition*, The MIT Press